Crash Course

Crash Course

IMAGINING
A BETTER
FUTURE FOR
PUBLIC
EDUCATION

Chris Whittle

RIVERHEAD BOOKS
A MEMBER OF PENGUIN GROUP (USA) INC.
NEW YORK   2005

RIVERHEAD BOOKS
Published by the Penguin Group
Penguin Group (USA) Inc., 375 Hudson Street, New York, New York 10014, USA • Penguin Group
(Canada), 90 Eglinton Avenue East, Suite 700, Toronto, Ontario M4P 2Y3, Canada (a division of Pearson
Penguin Canada Inc.) • Penguin Books Ltd, 80 Strand, London WC2R 0RL, England • Penguin Ireland,
25 St Stephen's Green, Dublin 2, Ireland (a division of Penguin Books Ltd) • Penguin Group (Australia),
250 Camberwell Road, Camberwell, Victoria 3124, Australia (a division of Pearson Australia Group Pty Ltd) •
Penguin Books India Pvt Ltd, 11 Community Centre, Panchsheel Park, New Delhi–110 017, India •
Penguin Group (NZ), Cnr Airborne and Rosedale Roads, Albany, Auckland 1310, New Zealand (a division
of Pearson New Zealand Ltd) • Penguin Books (South Africa) (Pty) Ltd, 24 Sturdee Avenue,
Rosebank, Johannesburg 2196, South Africa

Penguin Books Ltd, Registered Offices:
80 Strand, London WC2R 0RL, England

LIBRARY OF CONGRESS CATALOGING-IN-PUBLICATION DATA

Whittle, Chris.
Crash course : imagining a better future for public education / by Chris Whittle.
p.   cm.
Includes index.
ISBN 1-59448-902-5
1. Privatization in education—United States.   2. Public schools—United States.
3. Edison Schools Inc.   I. Title.
LB2806.36.W55   2005   2005046585
371.01'0973—dc22

Printed in the United States of America
1 3 5 7 9 10 8 6 4 2

This book is printed on acid-free paper. ∞

Book design by Lovedog Studio

While the author has made every effort to provide accurate telephone numbers and Internet addresses at
the time of publication, neither the publisher nor the author assumes any responsibility for errors, or for
changes that occur after publication. Further, the publisher does not have any control over and does not
assume any responsibility for author or third-party websites or their content.

To Herbert Whittle, Rita Whittle,
and Priscilla Rattazzi Whittle

Contents

FOREWORD:
PRACTICAL REVOLUTIONARY

P ractical revolutionaries are hard to come by, but we find
one here in Chris Whittle. Having watched him hone his
capacity for the unconventional in the world of media for almost
twenty years, I was intrigued when he turned his attention to our
nation's schools in the early 1990s. Would this be his undoing, or
would he contribute something very important to our times?
Would his opponents succeed in labeling him the bête noire of
public education, or would he actually help the country find a way
to save this treasured institution? Fifteen years and a number of
organizational near-death experiences later, we find him not only
standing but, in this book, seeing with a clarity achieved only by
those who can both paint the long view and muster the patience,
practicality, and perseverance to realize it. Readers who care about
our nation's children, take heed.

Crash Course is a book of great hope. Whittle believes America's public schools can become, in our lifetimes, the best on the
globe—indeed, even an export. He believes that we can transform

what some regard as our nation's Achilles' heel into a stunning competitive advantage. Yet what makes this book particularly special is that it is much more than a wish. It is a leader's guide, merging a compelling intellectual platform with a practitioner's understanding of the operational steps we must take to bring it about.

The press will be attracted to Whittle's original and readable ideas about how the school-day life of children will be (and should be) radically different in schools of the future. But I urge our country's political and educational leadership to focus equally on two more-complex concepts that underpin the thinking presented here—and that may be missed in the popular coverage. First, if our schools are to catch up with our times, their organization and provision must morph from largely local to an intricate collaboration of local governance and national capabilities. Local, public school districts and national, private providers must find a way to become partners. Only then, Whittle convincingly argues, will we see the development of modern educational systems and the powerful effects of research and development on the design of our schools. Only then will our schools be as effective and reliable as other sectors of our society. Second, our federal government must expand its role, moving beyond what some see as a national compliance agency. It must go beyond sewing labels on our schools to sowing the seeds of new designs. It must jump-start our country's enormous creative capacity, just as it once did with NASA and with the NIH.

Anytime an author ventures into ideologically supercharged territory with ideas that are frightening to a powerful status quo, harsh criticism is a certainty. That is particularly true when the author has a record of both stunning successes and embarrassing failures, as any daring innovator usually does. Having led both media organizations and a think tank, I know well how important concepts can be reduced to sound-bite status. Good ideas such as these deserve better. So I hope that this book will provoke not shallow debate but a substantive discussion of the important ideas presented here.

To wit: *Crash Course* advocates that our most talented teachers should be paid over $130,000 (nearly triple average current pay). Whittle actually shows us how we can do it—and without unrealistic tax increases. He says America must reorganize schools in ways that reduce the number of teachers we need, thus allowing pay to rise. Some opponents undoubtedly will label that "Half of Teachers to Be Fired" or "Class Sizes to Double." In fact, Whittle shows that this structural change can occur through simple teacher attrition and the introduction of more independent learning systems within schools. It is an idea that deserves to be discussed in total.

His idea that we must embrace the emergence of national and global schooling entities in order to advance R&D and other advantages of scale can easily be spun as "Schools to Become Chain Stores" or "McSchools." In fact, Whittle makes it clear that *local and public* authorities should continue to be in charge of our educational systems, with national-scale partners working *under* them.

His concept that students should play important roles in running our schools (and could learn much by doing so) could be spun as "Child Labor Returns." To do so mocks the centuries-old positive role that appropriate childhood responsibility has played in the American family and our most cherished institutions.

Whittle paints an exciting new role for the federal government in our nation's schools. Some will see that as "Big Government to Invade the Classroom." In fact, he sees the role of the federal government not as being the policeman of public education, but rather as promoting and supporting invention, something very difficult to achieve at the local level given the barriers of small-scale economies.

There will be those who question whether the private sector should be involved in public schooling at all. As Whittle built up Edison Schools, the slogan "Our Children Are Not for Sale" was frequently used. But I believe that private enterprise, entrepreneurship, competition, and the marketplace can help to make education—or any endeavor—more responsive to people's needs and more innovative. If new entities of national scale, be they nonprofit or for-profit, can help bring our schools to a higher level, should we not welcome that?

Finally, Whittle's imagination is large, and some may simply label his ideas as fantasies. Before rushing to such a conclusion, one might take a trip to the District of Columbia, where I now reside. It was here in 1991 that Whittle announced his plan to build Edison Schools. People were skeptical about his ideas, thinking them unrealistic. Today, with five significant D.C. campuses, over 5 percent of all students in the District are enrolled in a public school partnered with Edison—and the parents of many more children would like to have the same opportunity.

Those children are direct beneficiaries of Chris Whittle's ideas. So, too, will be the readers of this remarkable book.

WALTER ISAACSON
President
The Aspen Institute

FOREWORD:
A LARGER THREAT

Big problems require bold action. After nearly twenty-five years in public service, I have learned that courage to do things differently, followed by decisive action, is an essential ingredient if we are to resolve our most vexing public challenges.

For the past three and a half years, I have focused on one such challenge: the threat of terrorism to our nation. Terrorism is an all-encompassing challenge that demands the attention, innovation, and decisive action of all Americans. All levels of government, the private sector, and individual citizens have boldly resolved to tackle terrorism head-on. The newly created Department of Homeland Security has embraced the national imperative to change philosophy, relationships, and even the structure of proud, long-standing institutions to make us more effective against this threat. We drove significant positive innovation. And our nation is safer today as a result.

The challenge of transforming our public education system requires a similar level of national commitment. It demands acceptance of a similar notion that bold and dramatic actions are needed to effect the change the nation requires and our students deserve. Yet when it comes to our schools, we have too often shunned boldness for benign inertia. Despite consistent evidence of the widespread failure of our children, particularly children of color—failure that is both a human tragedy and a grave threat to our national prosperity—we react instead with numb acceptance. Resolve is replaced with resignation.

There have been some notable exceptions, however. I am proud that one of those exceptions began while I served as governor of Pennsylvania, shortly before the tragic events of September 11, 2001.

That summer, the school district of Philadelphia was on the brink of collapse. For decades, the eighth-largest school system in the United States had been failing to educate an extraordinarily high percentage of its 200,000 students. In dozens of Philadelphia schools, the percentage of children who had not yet acquired even basic proficiency in reading and math exceeded 90 percent. It was a profound level of public failure, with even more profound human implications for the children of Philadelphia. And the district was facing a financial crisis as well, a $200 million annual deficit.

As governor of Pennsylvania, I knew the challenge facing our state, these schools, and most important, the children required change that was both drastic and deep. Despite my belief that school districts should be locally controlled, there was no other choice but for the state to intervene and take responsibility for both academic and financial outcomes. I knew full well that state takeovers across the country had a history of failure. Most attempts simply replaced one educational bureaucracy with another, leaving performance in classrooms largely unchanged. If we were going to take over the Philadelphia schools, we knew we couldn't just assume control of operations. We had to make the systemic and philosophical changes necessary to help both students and schools excel. We had to make a difference.

That prompted my first meeting with Chris Whittle, founder and CEO of Edison Schools, then and now the nation's largest private partner of public schools. Whittle was considered visionary by some, and controversial by others, for his belief that the private sector could be harnessed to improve public education. I strongly shared his belief and was eager to talk.

By the time Whittle and I first met, he and his team had spent more than a decade and millions of dollars learning how to improve public schools. Their results were impressive, and so were they. They knew this would be the highest-profile urban education-reform effort in the nation. They knew the naysayers would be quick to criticize and even undermine their efforts. But they also knew it was an unprecedented opportunity to further the futures and dreams of a significant number of children. It was an unmatched forum to show how well their ideas worked. They were not naïve, but neither were they daunted.

Nor were we, so we acted. It was the largest state takeover of a school system in U.S. history. Edison was assigned perhaps the most challenging part of the effort—operation of twenty of the poorest-performing schools in Philadelphia with 12,000 children. No private company had ever been entrusted with the direct management of that many public schools.

As was expected, even before Edison took on its role, Whittle and his team were subjected to a year of staunch opposition. Edison's shares plummeted, losing, at one point, nearly $2 billion in value. Many feared that Edison would collapse under the political and financial pressure. But Whittle and his colleagues persevered.

They raised more capital, hunkered down, and focused on improving student performance. The results have been extraordinary. Just two years after they began, the Edison team had dramatically turned around the schools they were assigned. In the years before Edison arrived, annual achievement scores in these twenty schools were improving at less than 1 percentage point a year—a rate that would condemn thousands of children to squandered futures for generations to come. Last year, the rate of gain in those same schools averaged 10.5 percentage points. That is not just a statistic. It represents the restoration of human opportunity.

When Whittle introduced the idea of building a large, national system of public schools at the Washington Press Club in 1991, the boldness and originality of his ideas caught the attention of many. And in time, he showed that those ideas could work.

Now, after a decade of work in the trenches of America's toughest schools and fresh from his most important success in Philadelphia, he unveils his vision of what America must do next on the educational frontier.

Elected officials and candidates at all levels of government, parents, business leaders, teachers, and all others concerned about the future of our nation should read this book. It is a stark reminder of the imperative for boldness in education—of the painful reality that millions of children in our public schools are not receiving the education that they deserve, and that our country urgently needs them to acquire.

We need more policy and political leaders who will embrace bold, breakthrough thinking such as this when it comes to improving public education. They must have the resolve to resist the entrenched impediments to the success of our children. They must never forget that education is the ultimate tool of empowerment, and that it is our national responsibility to see that every child attending every public school is so empowered. All of us must commit to the hard work ahead so that all of our children have an equal chance to succeed in a country whose own success depends on that very outcome.

This book shows us the way.

Tom Ridge
Former U.S. Secretary of
Homeland Security
Washington, D.C.
April 20, 2005

Introduction

Some people like to build new houses. I'm a renovation man. I'm drawn to the good bones, the distinctive features, and the time-chiseled character of an old home. I've rehabbed residences since college, from a Depression-era two-room log cabin in Tennessee (where I lived for twenty years) to a rambling apartment in one of New York's oldest apartment buildings, the 1880s Dakota. Nothing excites me more than the mess, confusion, and potential of a full-tilt renovation site.

From a relatively young age, I have enjoyed walking into a pre-existing structure and imagining it reconfigured, sometimes radically so, but with the irreplaceable vintage parts and characteristics maintained and reused. I begin such a process by envisioning all the floors removed and all the interior walls down, save the load-bearing ones. In my mind's eye, only the exterior walls and roof remain (with even the fenestration and pitch open to reconsideration). It's as if the structure becomes a large empty box, beginning at the basement floor and extending to the rafters with no impairments, no "givens." Then I begin to imagine how to bring together seamlessly the virtues and beauty of the original with the best of new discoveries since.

It takes patience. Serious renovations can consume years, whereas a whole new structure might be built in half the time or less. Many find the process exceedingly tedious. But I've always thought the end product was worth it: age enriched by youth; one room where four may have stood, or vice versa; flat screens encased in worn brick; a weathered floorboard in a modern kitchen; technology brought to previous centuries.

Over the past decade and a half, I have approached our system of public education with this same sensibility—a desire to imagine what could be instead of what has been and then to synthesize the best of both.

If education were a house, it would be our nation's second-largest (health care being the greatest). The K–12 public portion of it is a nation-spanning network of sprawling organizations and structures, the vast scale of which is not widely understood. Roughly one American in five spends the *entire day* within it, either as a student or as an adult who works there. American public education enrolls or employs 54 million people, nearly the population of Great Britain. It is effectively a country within our country. It would require a mortgage of roughly $1 trillion to build it from scratch—90,000 *significant* facilities and countless smaller ones. Its square footage approaches that of a thousand World Trade Centers. And operating it costs us, *every school hour,* a staggering $350 million. The *average* American household pays nearly $4,000 every year in taxes to support our public schools, whether it has children in them or not.

We should be immensely proud of the vastness of this "structure" and its great accomplishments. Public education is the embodiment of our nation's commitment to equal opportunity. And within this immense entity, there are grand, brilliant features that we should never forsake. But there also are aspects of which we should be ashamed. Dimly lit areas, so to speak: the unkempt rooms, flooded basements, neglected attics, and outbuildings, the contents and results of which are a national embarrassment. Both realities are true.

In 1989, I became part of this great educational structure, perhaps as an uninvited guest. Since then, I've been trying to imagine it organized differently—not physically but programmatically—in a way that would better serve our nation's children, conserve its greatness, help it make the transition to modern times, and yes, build an important new company, Edison Schools, to boot. My engagement has not been a passing fancy, having already required fifteen years of my life. Yet I am far from finished, and I hope to spend another fifteen or twenty years on what has become my life's work: to assist in the renovation of American public education.

Today, Edison touches and improves the lives of 270,000 children—all *public* school students who attend free of charge—in nineteen states plus the District of Columbia, and also in Great Britain. Edison manages 157 public schools in the United States, with an enrollment of 70,000 students—nearly 80 percent of whom are below the poverty line and over 85 percent of whom are children of color. If it were an actual public school system, Edison would be the forty-seventh-largest in the country, roughly similar in size to the school systems serving Denver, Colorado, or Cleveland, Ohio. Additionally, Edison provides partial services (tutoring, summer schools, etc.) to another 200,000 students at 900 other locations in the United States and Britain. As a company, it is a $400+ million entity, with a full-time staff of over

6,000 and a part-time staff of thousands more. And it has spawned a new category that now includes dozens of competitors.

This book is profoundly informed by my years at Edison Schools. That time "on site," if you will, may make what I have to say worthy of your consideration. But this book is not about Edison, as important as I believe that story to be, and as much as the thinking within this book might shape Edison's future.

Instead, I view *Crash Course* as a midpoint in the history of an important idea, an idea that extends far beyond the boundaries of Edison Schools. That idea is to take the great old house of public education, the very portal of the American dream, and move it dramatically forward—utilizing, as a major new ingredient, the world-class vibrancy and inventiveness of America's private sector. I see this book as that idea's pause to find fresh horses, gain new perspectives, and make midcourse corrections. This book tries to capture what I've seen and learned about that idea—particularly lessons I've learned about the future of large-scale private-sector involvement in the creation, management, and improvement of our public schools.

Here's a quick guide to *Crash Course*.

Chapter 1 is a wake-up call. It describes, in ways the reader probably has not seen, the decades-long, national crisis within a large portion of our educational system. Its purpose is to convince you that it is not our children who are failing, but we who are failing millions of them. It does not bash American public education but calls all of us on the carpet for letting significant portions of this treasured institution languish. Chapter 2 discusses what I view as the primary factor in this dysfunction: the unparalleled fragmentation of our public education system that leads inescapably to an utterly inadequate national investment in creative solutions. To say this a bit differently, the mere structure of our educational system causes a failure of national imagination. Chapter 3 shows how and why prior efforts to confront this massive issue, despite good intent, have altered the landscape far less than one might wish.

Part II, the intermezzo between analysis and vision, consists of only one chapter. Its purpose is to establish, briefly, my credentials so you can better judge the future of education that I will later propose. I provide a short history of my work in the vineyards of public education and show how that experience serves as the footing for the future I see—a future that I hope will make America's public schools the envy of the world, just as our universities are.

Part III is that future, in both micro and macro versions. It invites you to imagine with me what is possible for public schooling, in the United States and abroad. You might be surprised by my optimism. Part III begins at the school-building level, highlighting new elements we must bring to our schools. This section also argues that these enhancements are not idle pipe dreams, devoid of economic and operational integrity. It demonstrates that we can bring all these advancements to our children, largely with resources we already have.

We then move from the school-level view to a macro picture of how schooling in the future could be provided. The book describes how school systems, both large and small, can radically reshape themselves over the coming twenty-five years—and it introduces the idea of major schooling providers and how they can emerge, to the profound betterment of public education, between now and 2030.

Part IV is a message to America's leadership. In my view, the changes proposed in this book are as inevitable as the fall of the Berlin Wall. But the question is, When? How many more millions of our children will not realize what America offers? The answer will be driven by two factors: an increase in political courage and vision and a corresponding decrease in resistance by parochial interests. This section particularly calls for a new level of leadership (and investment) at the federal level and lays out a blueprint for how that might occur. It ends with letters and respectful but unsolicited advice to those who are in the best position to accelerate this new reality, something we have promised but not delivered to 15 million of our children, the great majority of whom are poor and of color.

PART I

The Problem, the Cause, and Failed Solutions

CHAPTER 1

15 Million Children Lost, Just Not Yours

What would the federal government do if every day a thousand commercial airplanes crashed? How would the nation react if every day there were a power failure equivalent to the one that struck the Northeast in 2003? How would the press react if the infant mortality rate increased thirtyfold from current levels? What would *Consumer Reports* have to say if every day 40 million U.S. automobiles simply failed to start?

My guess is that you instantly dismiss such scenarios as absurd. Even though each scenario presumes a failure rate of "only" 20 to 30 percent, you probably view them as too far-fetched to merit serious consideration. In each case you intuitively know that the country simply would not accept such failure. In every one of the examples, we *expect and receive* near-perfect performance. In the safety of airline flights, the availability of electricity, the safety of childbirth at our local hospitals, and the performance of our cars, we expect well over 99 percent reliability, just as we do in hundreds of other areas of our lives.

Now ask yourself this question: How would the nation react if 15 million of our children were required, every day, to go to schools that did not even teach them to read well? Tragically, this question is not hypothetical. And we don't have to guess how we would react. We are witnesses. We *are* sending 15 million of our children, most of whom are poor and of color, to schools that, by government statistics, are significantly failing to deliver on a promise this democracy proudly makes to all its citizens: an equal start. And if you judge our country not on what it says, not on what it hopes or plans, but rather on how it actually has responded to this devastating loss of human potential, then our record is a national embarrassment. So much so that it begs more questions: If we have known about this for over two decades, why have we let it go on? If we expect and receive near perfection in so many aspects of our society and lives, why do we tolerate such systematic failure in the performance of a significant number of our nation's schools? Why do we apply a lower standard for the future and well-being of our children than we apply to clearly less important things, such as our cars? To find out, we must first look more closely at the problem itself.

In a meeting with Pennsylvania legislators in November 2002, I handed out a chart of the mathematics performance of twenty of Philadelphia's lowest-performing schools. To my surprise, the lawmakers looked at the chart in rapt attention as we talked. They seemed shocked, as if in disbelief. I remember saying to myself, "Perhaps I've finally found a way to convey the magnitude of the problem."

You would think that educational inadequacy is easy enough to communicate. It is not. In nearly fifteen years working with political leaders and the media, I've observed that statistics on educational problems bounce off audiences as if failure for some students is inevitable. Whatever the cause of this resistance to data, the chart that day in Harrisburg seemed to have an impact. So I offer it here as a way to begin the review of an educational tragedy that has been unfolding for decades in our country. This chart represents the percentage of children classified as "proficient" on Pennsylvania's state math exam in twenty Philadelphia schools before my company, Edison Schools, began managing them. Take a look:

PERCENTAGE OF STUDENTS PASSING 2002 PENNSYLVANIA MATH EXAM IN 20 PHILADELPHIA SCHOOLS*

School A	1.1%	School K	5.8%
School B	2.4%	School L	6.9%
School C	2.7%	School M	6.9%
School D	2.9%	School N	7.1%
School E	3.0%	School O	8.9%
School F	3.8%	School P	9.2%
School G	4.8%	School Q	10.6%
School H	5.1%	School R	10.7%
School I	5.3%	School S	11.0%
School J	5.5%	School T	11.6%

*If school is elementary, scores are fifth grade. If middle school, eighth grade.

No, you are not misreading it. In the *best* of these schools, 88.4 percent were not proficient in math in 2002. In the worst, 98.9 percent failed to achieve proficiency. "Proficiency"—a category used to describe satisfactory performance on various state and federal achivement tests—does not mean a student is great, just solid.

The typical school in the above list has about 600 students. That means, in School A, for example, of 600 students, only seven can function in math at acceptable levels. To think of it in another way, in a first grade of 125 students, only one or two are proficient. In airline crashes we are accustomed to the concept of "no survivors." It is not a phrase you would think to apply to our schools.

But let's not pick on Philadelphia. Here's a chart of New York State's twenty lowest-performing schools in math for 2004, looked at on the same measure, just using New York State standards:

PERCENTAGE OF STUDENTS PASSING 2004 NEW YORK STATE MATH EXAM IN 20 LOWEST-PERFORMING SCHOOLS			
School A	0.0%	School K	0.0%
School B	0.0%	School L	0.0%
School C	0.0%	School M	0.0%
School D	0.0%	School N	1.3%
School E	0.0%	School O	3.1%
School F	0.0%	School P	5.3%
School G	0.0%	School Q	6.2%
School H	0.0%	School R	6.3%
School I	0.0%	School S	6.4%
School J	0.0%	School T	7.1%

Yes, the performance is even more alarming than in the Philadelphia schools. In thirteen schools in the state of New York, *not one student was proficient in math.* In case you are wondering whether this is a phenomenon related to mathematics, the answer is no.

Perhaps, you might be thinking, this is predominantly an urban or Northeastern issue. Unfortunately, no again. Here are the results for the twenty lowest-performing schools in South Carolina in 2004:

PERCENTAGE OF STUDENTS PASSING 2004 SOUTH CAROLINA MATH EXAM IN 20 LOWEST-PERFORMING SCHOOLS			
School A	0.0%	School K	5.5%
School B	0.0%	School L	5.5%
School C	2.1%	School M	6.2%
School D	2.8%	School N	6.4%
School E	4.0%	School O	6.4%
School F	4.7%	School P	6.7%
School G	4.7%	School Q	7.0%
School H	5.3%	School R	7.1%
School I	5.3%	School S	7.2%
School J	5.5%	School T	7.2%

And though my focus in these examples is largely on urban systems, let's not forget what happens in many of our most successful schools, where students of exceptional capability perform only at average levels. In other words, even America's best students are not keeping pace in many international comparisons.

It took me a while to understand why the above charts were compelling whereas other data seems not to be. The reason: This approach forces the reader to consider *that the school is the issue, not the children.* The reader intuitively understands the unlikelihood that only a handful of children would be intellectually capable of scoring at proficient levels in math or reading if a school were actually effective in teaching them.

So ask yourself this: How many American children are not achieving a level of success critical to modern life? Answer: *about 15 million.* Try to get your mind around the scale of this for a moment. America has more children who are below basic levels of achievement *than England has children.*

Nor is this some conspiracy of state data. The U.S. Department of Education periodically conducts an assessment of the knowledge of students in various subject areas called the National Assessment of Educational Progress (NAEP). There are four categories of achievement on NAEP: advanced, proficient, basic, and below basic. On the 1992 NAEP, 38 percent of our fourth-graders were "below basic"—two full levels *below* proficiency—in reading. Eleven years later (a whole generation of children), on the 2003 NAEP, a nearly identical 37 percent were "below basic." At this glacier-like rate of improvement, it would take America over 400 years just to get its fourth-graders to "basic" in reading.

Still, these are just numbers. Think about it, then, as if each of these 15 million children were, say, *your son or daughter.* Try to imagine your child's life and future. Because reading is the building block for all future learning, if he or she were "below basic" in reading, the entire school experience, from kindergarten to high school, would be immensely frustrating. There would be a growing sense of failure due to the inability to read class textbooks—much less excel academically. There is a high likelihood he or she would drop out of school—a somewhat rational response, if you think about it. Your son would have a greater chance of doing time than spending time in college, a premise supported by the fact that more African-American men are in prison than in college. Your child's career, if you want to call it that, would probably be menial employment, at best.

If these were even remotely the prospects for your child, chances are you would mobilize to make sure that it did not happen. But for some reason, we as a nation do not mobilize on behalf of the underserved children in our schools. We have talked about doing something; we have planned to do something; we have started to do something, but we have not followed through—and we most certainly have not succeeded. As a nation, we are acting as if these are not our children. Educational failure for many of our children has become so commonplace and been with us so long that we have lost our sense of outrage.

Some might say that I am going too far here. They would say that the nation has been mobilizing for two decades to deal with this issue. To be sure, we have enough new educational-improvement initiatives to fill a library. Indeed, individual schools have made remarkable progress, and some whole systems have moved forward dramatically. But these initiatives and instances cannot mask the reality of our own test scores. What I'm saying is that we must grade our own paper as we grade those of our children—not on effort, not on whether they got one or two questions right, not on whether they want to pass, not on whether we like educators and know them to be well intentioned, but rather on the overall result. And there we deserve the same grade we are giving so many millions of children. How can we say otherwise when the majority of children in thousands of schools are below proficient levels of performance?

America clearly has two daunting educational issues: the failure of large numbers of our schools, which is now old news, and *our failure to deal with it.*

So why? Why does the greatest nation in the history of mankind allow roughly 30 percent of its children to languish in functional illiteracy? Why does a nation that has gone to the moon and Mars, that finds the time and resources to invent such things as Viagra, Prozac, Rogaine, and all things fat- and now carbohydrate-free, why can't we find a way to ensure that 99 percent of our children at least learn to read?

Let's *not* start by blaming this situation on public education. Public schools are a government agency, and the government is our collective agency. The culprits here, if there are culprits, are less-than-visionary political leadership and less-than-mobilized citizenry. Why might that be?

Here are three reasons for your consideration. First, we don't believe it can be done. Down deep, lots of people believe this is "just the way it is," similar to some people's view that there will always be poverty. If we do not believe in the potential to solve a problem, how likely is it that we will really act? Second, people of power and privilege don't experience the problem. If there is no ownership of an issue "at the top" of our society, will there really be a national motivation to fix it? Third, we've lacked vision in our efforts to change this. Our efforts bear no resemblance to what this country is capable of when it truly mobilizes.

Let's look at each.

We Don't Believe

One day I was meeting with a high-ranking educational figure who I'll leave unnamed, for reasons that will become apparent. We were discussing whether Edison could help some particularly troubled schools where well over 90 percent of the children were not proficient on state exams. The children were almost all poor and almost all of color.

As we were reviewing the statistics on student achievement, I happened to note that almost no children were performing at advanced levels. The official said something to the effect of "That's never going to happen. Our interest is to get them to basic levels." The Edison representatives in the room were stunned. A serious educator was effectively saying that poor children of color could not be educated beyond the basics, that their circumstances could not be overcome. It is easy to call this racism, and in some cases I'm sure that is exactly what it is. But it is important to go beyond that interpretation. Let me try.

A number of people in America believe some percentage of our children will simply fail. They believe that if we "grade on the curve" nationally, there will always be a distribution of performance. If you look at it from this point of view, you can see why some people would not be particularly agitated by the fact that so many children are not proficient. You can also see how they would "blame" this failure not on schools but on "circumstances," or even on the children.

Logical as this view may seem, it is not correct. Let's pierce it in a number of ways.

First, if we were to "grade on a curve," the "curve" should exist in all schools. That is, if 30 percent of all children were going to fail, then 30 percent, more or less, of the children in *every* school should fail—if, of course, every school were doing an equal job. As the charts of school performance earlier in this chapter show, such is not the case. Certain schools have virtually no success. It would be easy to conclude that children in the neighborhoods of failing schools simply can't perform. That *is* racist and also untrue. Overwhelming evidence demonstrates that *if schools in these neighborhoods did their job,* the children would do theirs. Let me give you just one case in point.

In 2000 the state of Maryland seized control of three of the lowest-performing elementary schools in the city of Baltimore and asked Edison Schools to turn them around under a five-year management agreement. Located in some of Baltimore's most poverty-ridden and drug-infested neighborhoods, these schools were full of students who were failing—and had been failing for years. So what did we do? We changed almost everything. Out went the old books, the old technology, and yes, many of the prior staff who had been part of a culture of low expectations. In came new books, new technology, and many new team members— men and women who universally believed these children could perform. Just one thing did not change: the children attending. And what happened? In three years, a combined effort of the state of Maryland, Edison, teachers, parents, and the children themselves moved these schools dramatically forward. In the best case, Montebello Elementary, student achievement *tripled.* Look what happened to proficiency rates in reading and math in the following chart:

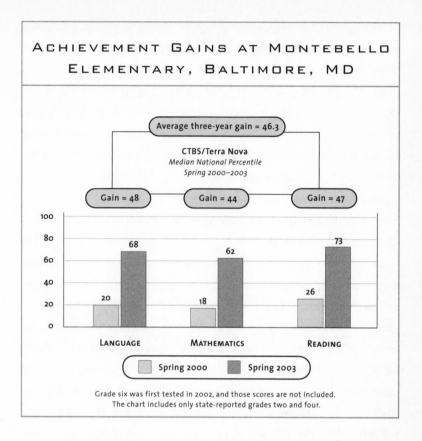

ACHIEVEMENT GAINS AT MONTEBELLO
ELEMENTARY, BALTIMORE, MD

Average three-year gain = 46.3

CTBS/Terra Nova
Median National Percentile
Spring 2000–2003

Gain = 48   Gain = 44   Gain = 47

Grade six was first tested in 2002, and those scores are not included.
The chart includes only state-reported grades two and four.

You might remember the movie *Stand and Deliver,* in which a group of underprivileged high school students in California performed far better than expected for students from their circumstances on the AP calculus exam. In the film, which was based on real events, educational authorities questioned whether the students' AP test scores were valid. The students agreed to be retested—and all achieved similar scores the second time around. In the case of Montebello, the students' test scores were so much higher than before that the state of Maryland retested them. And guess what? Montebello students did even better in the retest than in the original! We did nothing at Montebello that cannot be done in *every* failing school in America. By the way, we did it with financial resources similar to those of other Baltimore elementary schools.

So the idea that some significant percentage of our nation's children cannot achieve proficiency is just wrong. Virtually all of them can *if* they attend effective schools. Everyone cannot be at the top of the class. Not all will go to Harvard, not all will even go to college, but virtually all can be literate. All can have the "thorough and efficient" education that most state constitutions require but do not deliver to all. We don't distribute airline safety, electricity, or auto safety "on a curve." Whether you fly from New York to Los Angeles in first class, business class, or coach, you will arrive there safely. The reliability of electrical service is, more or less, the same whether you live in Greenwich or the Bronx. And cars, no matter what the sticker price, have a similar degree of reliability. In the area of health, we don't expect every child to be an Olympic athlete, but we know that virtually every birth will occur safely. So it should be in education. Virtually every child *can* reach proficiency. It is educational malpractice that we allow otherwise. In the schools portrayed earlier in this chapter, the children were not failing. Their schools were. And more important, we were failing, for letting such an injustice continue.

We Don't Own the Problem

At a failing school in California that Edison was asked to manage, teachers were asked in a survey before we arrived if they would send their own children to the school. Most said no. In Chicago, nearly 40 percent of all public school teachers send their children to private schools. In some American cities, school boards pass regulations *requiring* that teachers live in the city where they teach.

Without such a rule, the vast percentage of teachers would live in neighboring suburbs so they could send their children to what they consider to be better public schools. Mayors of America's largest cities routinely send their children not to public schools but to private ones. The *Washington Post* reported in 1997 that no members of the U.S. Senate or Congress or any senior administrative figures sent their children to D.C.'s public schools. And in what has to be viewed as one of his most politically courageous acts, Bill Clinton, a man who owed his presidential election in no small part to public teacher unions, sent his daughter to a $20,000-per-year private school.

The point? In cities with largely low-performing schools, people with power and wealth have routinely exercised a choice that those in poverty do not have: to move where public schools are better or to "pay twice," their taxes *and* their private school tuition. There are two consequences of such actions: *their* children get a better education and *they* no longer "own" the problem that exists in a significant number of our public schools.

A good way to gain perspective on this issue is to imagine its opposite. What if private schools were prohibited in New York City and "flight to the suburbs" was disallowed as well? (Sound particularly outrageous and un-American? To poor people in New York, these conditions effectively exist already as a result of their economic position.) What would happen? You can bet that New York City's public schools would improve quickly. Why? Because people in power would have to experience the public school reality. They simply would not abide the level of failure that exists in so many schools. They would respond with the same kind of focused outrage and zeal that would be triggered by rampant failure rates in airplane travel, electricity transmission, or childbirth safety. Money would be no object. Political alliances would crumble. Personal allegiances would be shoved to the back seat.

This particular lack of ownership can be seen as a sin of omission. But that once again is giving ourselves more slack than we typically give to others. If we are really to examine this problem—our lack of dealing with it, that is—then we have to look beyond simple omission. We have to look, as Jack Nicholson's character said in the courtroom monologue in *A Few Good Men,* in "places you don't talk about at parties."

Could it be that what we are doing is actually aggressively in the wrong, if ever so nicely hidden? I agree with Freud that very little in life is an accident, that we get what we want and do what we want, even if we say otherwise, even if it appears that we dislike our circumstance or say we are dismayed by someone else's. If you give that point of view some merit, then you must ask if there is intentionality in the state of affairs of our schools. To some it may seem unlikely that a nation founded on equality would institutionalize the reverse. But that same nation embraced slavery for nearly a hundred years, or nearly half its history. Do we think we have completely erased that "gene pool"? Is it just accidental that virtually all the children in failing schools in America are children of color and poverty? Is it possible that somewhere inside us *we don't want everyone to be well educated*? Is it possible that we're actually worried about how America would function with 100 percent literacy? If everyone read well, would that somehow destabilize the hierarchy we now have?

We are not an evil people. But we have been blind to our faults before.

We Don't See the Solution

If we don't believe all children can reach certain levels of proficiency, and if we don't own and experience the problem of a significant portion of our educational system (and perhaps even secretly need it), then it is not surprising that we have not exercised a great deal of vision to find a solution.

Compare and contrast. Compare the effort this country has put into building its armed forces to the effort we have put into K–12 education. On the surface, we now spend roughly the same on schools as on the military—over $400 billion for each. Looked at another way, however: we spend in the aggregate far more for each active-duty person in the military than we spend for each public school teacher. But the issue is far beyond the allocation of dollars to those in "combat." It is more about how we have applied our national creativity. Look at how a soldier goes into battle: trained constantly, connected by every imaginable communication mechanism integrated with satellites, supported by every type of advanced weapon, protected by body armor, often saved by mobile medicine, and on and on. Contrast that to how a teacher goes to war against ignorance: with ivory-tower, not on-the-battlefield, training; in a classroom remarkably similar to that of the Middle Ages; with communication often via the pay phone down the hall; with computers only sometimes, and then frequently in need of repair or upgrade. Is that an indication of vision?

Look at what we did to build the U.S. Interstate system. Look at NASA. Have we approached our schooling with such focus and ingenuity? (While we're at it, look at how we have engaged the private sector in *all* the above initiatives as an active, supporting partner. More on that later.)

And I'm just comparing our efforts in education to other government work right now. When you look at the private sector's efforts to increase performance to high levels, the contrasts are even greater. Where in the field of education would you find the equivalent of the pharmaceutical giants that invest billions annu-

ally in R&D to advance our health? Where in the field of education would you find comparables to the labs of IBM, Intel, and
Apple? Where in education would you see the creativity of our
entertainment industry?

How can we say we have approached education with true national resolve? If we had, we would have fixed the problem.

CHAPTER 2

The Last Great Cottage Industry

When I grew up in the 1950s in Etowah, Tennessee, a town of 3,700, equidistant from Chattanooga and Knoxville, almost every enterprise was locally owned and operated. There was a local hardware store, a local bank, local grocery stores, a local motel, a local newspaper, a local drive-in for burgers, and a local department store. As I think back, I can remember only two establishments that had "national ties"—the car dealerships (Chevrolet, Ford, and Chrysler) and the gas stations (Gulf, Texaco, and Esso).

Like everything else, our schools were local. We had one elementary school, one middle school, and one high school, educating a total of about 1,200 students. They made up the Etowah School District, with its own superintendent and school board (my dad was its president for a while). I went to these schools for twelve years, as did everyone else in town. The only other choice was to move—there were no private or parochial schools.

Today, fifty years later, Etowah has progressed with the rest of the country. Nationally branded car dealerships and gas stations remain as then, but regional or national banks have typically replaced local ones. Hardware stores struggle to compete against Home Depots and Lowe's. National retailers fill nearby malls. Local motels have succumbed to competition from the likes of Days Inn. Grocery stores are now giant Krogers and Safeways. And individual drive-ins have given way to McDonald's or Hardee's.

As you read this, you may feel, like many, a sense of loss, a sense that family-run, small-town America has been replaced by charmless chains brought to us by big business. While that may be so, it is important to remember that this transition has been chosen by consumers rather than imposed by business. In each case, customers decided to go to these new establishments because they liked what was offered there. They traded their old world, which certainly had its merits, for what offered more value, more convenience, or more choice.

Such a trade has not been made in schools, though, because no options have been offered there. Across the country, schools remain relentlessly local. Although the schools that I attended have been torn down (they were pretty far gone even when I was there), the Etowah School District still remains with its own school board and superintendent. The biggest change is that Etowah elementary students now "graduate" to schools run by McMinn County. The school structure remains much as it was in all the neighboring towns. Virtually every school district we played in football is still around. (I can almost remember the schedule.) And every district still has its own superintendent, its own school board, and its own district staff.

Over the past century in America, virtually every category of goods and services has dramatically shifted from local enterprises to national and regional ones. American education stands as an island, impervious to this broad trend. The twenty largest school districts educate only 10 percent of the nation's children. Although size in other sectors has resulted in innovation and improved cost efficiency, size in schooling is widely viewed as a problem—a view supported by the fact that our largest school districts are often some of our worst-performing. In fact, many reform efforts over the past two decades have sought to reduce the scale of schooling organizations in the belief that "systems" stifle school performance and innovation. The move to "site-based decision making" in school districts and the creation of charter schools grew from a view held by many people that school systems were oppressive, ineffective central governments. In short, we have argued that unlike almost every other service institution in the nation, schools will function better if they are organized into smaller and more fragmented systems.

A different way to consider the same thing is to contrast the largest "schooling organizations" with the largest organizations in other categories of service. Here are the top five companies in America compared with the top five school districts:

A MATTER OF SCALE

A COMPARISON OF AMERICA'S TOP 5 COMPANIES TO THE TOP 5 SCHOOL DISTRICTS*

Wal-Mart Stores	$288	New York City	$12.1
Exxon Mobil	$271	Los Angeles Unified	$6.4
General Motors	$194	City of Chicago	$3.8
Ford Motor	$172	Dade County	$2.9
General Electric	$152	Broward County	$2.0

*Revenue in billions. Company revenue for 2005; district revenue for 2000–2001.

Wal-Mart is 24 times larger than New York City's school system, our largest system of schools. General Electric, our fifth-largest company, is nearly 13 times the size of the New York school system. You might think such a differential exists because these business categories are so much larger than K–12 public education. Surprise: that is not the case. As noted earlier in this book, we spend over $400 billion per year to educate our children from kindergarten through high school. The problem is that our schools have been organized differently from the way other mass-scale product or service providers in America have been organized.

I say "we have organized our schools" as if this were some well-considered judgment. Perhaps it was, one hundred years ago, but today's political leaders did not explicitly make this decision. They inherited it. The way our schools are controlled and provided came about over a century ago, when individual cities began to form the first public school systems. As each new town or city sprang up, it followed the example of its neighboring town down the way. Compared with virtually any other category of importance in America, K–12 education is hugely fragmented.

So ask yourself whether this highly splintered, highly local organization of the educational process helped or hurt the quality of our schools. Can the severe problems described in the first chapter of this book be attributed, at least in part, to the way our school systems are structured?

When I first became involved in America's schools and knew little about them, I thought the answer to that question was yes. Today, after fifteen years in the trenches of education, I have no doubt. The organization of our schools essentially makes them America's last great cottage industry. They are asked to solve problems that even an organization of great scale would find daunting. To state it simply, scale brings critical new forces into play, powerful forces that, in my view, we need in order to solve our educational crisis. Is scale the only missing ingredient? No. But it is a gating factor, a precondition that, left as is, will undermine all other factors that we bring to bear on this issue. While some desire a return to the one-room schoolhouse, where teachers confront and solve all problems in independent and solitary glory, I see a future in which teachers are supercharged by a powerful, large-scale systemic infrastructure, one that enables them to be the critical, central ingredient of education.

What exactly is the power of scale? Too often, proponents of scale talk about it as "consolidation" that is virtuous for its cost efficiencies. Those efficiencies are real, but this view misses the larger point. The power of scale—and the only reason we should care about its impact on education—rests in the way it gives birth to certain types of creativity, in its capacity to make large-scale research and development possible.

R&D has been the engine of the most exciting transformations in our world. R&D has enabled us to have transportation systems and medical systems and power systems that routinely deliver success rates of 99 percent. R&D leads us down two great roads to quality: better design and better systems—ingredients American schools are sorely lacking precisely because of their fragmented organization. School design, by the way, includes the design of every aspect of a school, from curriculum to schedule to organization to budget.

When I meet with the head of a major U.S. school district, I typically ask this question: "How large is your R&D budget?" The response is always a laugh ("Are you kidding?") or a puzzled look ("I don't know what you mean"). The reality is simply this: School districts don't have R&D budgets, or in those few cases where they do, the budgets are microscopically small in the scheme of serious R&D. Contrast this to the reality in other sectors of American life. The following chart shows the revenue and related

R&D budgets for three of America's largest companies. Are Ford, GE, and IBM—or any of the other serious businesses in the country—wasting that money? Or have they rightly determined that such spending is necessary to maintain their ability to improve and compete in a rapidly changing world? And if such investment is critical in these categories, how can it be irrelevant to the shaping of minds?

SERIOUS R&D			
	TOTAL REVENUE	R&D SPENDING	% OF REVENUE
Ford	$172B	$7.4B	4.3%
GE	$152B	$3B	2.0%
IBM	$87B	$5B	5.7%

Some would argue that there is a great deal of research on schooling, pointing to our colleges of education. I would respectfully argue that those institutions do not come close to providing the kind of R&D that schools need in order to improve. My emphasis is not on the R in R&D but on the D. Research is not development. As important as it is, research is generally examination, illumination, discussion. Development is all about solutions—execution, integration, workability. Education is rife with research but starved for development.

But what of textbook manufacturers? Aren't they doing a lot of development in the educational sector? Yes, they are, but in limited areas. They would be the equivalent of Goodyear's or Firestone's advancement of tires in the automotive world. Critical components, yes. Good work, yes. But they did not lead us from the Model T to the BMW 7 Series.

Speaking of cars, though all cars still have five wheels, four on the ground and one to steer with, there have been enormous improvements over the cars of a century ago. The combined annual R&D budgets of GM, Ford, and DaimlerChrysler total nearly $20 billion a year. This type of spending has led to greater safety (seat belts, air bags, roll cages, better visibility, better headlights); greater efficiency (average gas mileage has been much improved since the car was introduced); greater comfort (adjustable seats, air conditioning, heated seats, improved suspension, and all manner of ergonomic improvements); greater pleasure (most cars today are rolling entertainment centers, with sound and video systems better integrated than those in our homes); and greater convenience (car phones, navigation systems, even rolling OnStar concierge services!). Car manufacturers have made such improvements while holding the price of an entry-level car basically the same, in current dollars, as when Henry Ford first introduced the Model T!

Now let's think about how our schools, without the benefit of serious R&D, have changed in the past century. Shall we begin with something as simple as how schools approach time—the school calendar, a well-known joke to those familiar with American education? Our almost universal school calendar of nine months was developed in agrarian times, so children could work in the fields during the summer. News flash: Most don't do that anymore. (It is also important to note that there is considerable research showing that this calendar significantly impairs educational progress, because children forget a great deal during the summer break.) The common 6-hour-and-30-minute school day, so wildly inconvenient for working parents, was developed in an era when Mom was home with cookies and milk at 2:30. Schools' lack of responsiveness to this societal trend has almost single-handedly created generations of "latchkey" children and caused most of us, in one way or another, to pay for before- and after-school services that would be more convenient and efficient if built into the regular school day.

Then think of our "calendar" in a broader sense—when in life formal schooling for children begins and ends. In 1930 most children began school at age six and ended at age eighteen. There is very little difference in that today, with less than half of U.S. states even providing full-day kindergarten. Our children, however, are not the same as they were in 1930. One physiological example: the age of puberty for girls has declined substantially in the last century. And sociologically, our children—both early in their childhood and later—are exposed to so much more. Would it not make sense, then, to begin formal education much earlier and end it sooner, effectively "shifting forward" the thirteen years of schooling we provide by a couple of years? If you want to think about why R&D is required for change, just consider the complexities of this one change. Without a serious R&D function, how would a major school district actually deal with changing its entire approach to time?

Our schools remain stuck in the past in ways far beyond years, days, and cycles. Back when I was forming Edison Schools, I volunteered for two years as a tutor in a New York City school, just to understand more what occurred in classrooms. To make a phone call, one had to go to the teachers' lounge and use a pay phone. Nearly a century after the invention of the phone, our school design did not incorporate the ability for a teacher to speak easily with a parent—or for a parent to speak easily with a teacher. In 1995, 88 percent of U.S. classrooms still had no phone. After I launched Channel One, a company that provided educational TV programming, in 1989, we discovered that only 6 percent of U.S.

classrooms had a television, fifty years after this marvel of communications was introduced.

Schools were somewhat more responsive to the computer age but at first viewed computers as something to learn about as opposed to something to learn with. Though virtually all schools have some computers and a level of network connectivity, when you compare their technological infrastructure with that of modern businesses, it is still primitive. Where businesses view robust information technology (IT) as a must, many schools still view it as an aspiration. The average U.S. secretary is far more technologically equipped than the average U.S. teacher. Why? The integration of technology doesn't just happen. It comes from R&D capacity, the ability to both understand and integrate new technology. It is no secret that most larger enterprises are far more technologically advanced than their smaller counterparts. It comes from R&D.

The area where education remains perhaps most trapped in the past is its data systems. Compared with virtually every other sector of our society, schools are data-starved. In the 1980s I used to visit the Federal Express headquarters in Memphis. I noticed in the lobby there was a "white board" on which FedEx posted, daily, the number of packages picked up the prior evening and, in percentage terms, the number delivered by 10:30 that morning. If you were there after 10:30, the number was always filled in at something over 99.9 percent. I was amazed not only at the success in delivery but also that they *knew* so quickly. It's no different at retail establishments like Gap. Every evening marketers know how many sweaters of what color they sold during the day. And if you are a modern-day airline pilot, at your fingertips are hundreds of types of "real-time" information—from your exact location to your rate of climb, airspeed, and fuel burn, and the function of all critical elements of a plane. Today's planes even include a new information system called TCAST, which advises a pilot of the location of every other aircraft in his vicinity. If he comes too close, it advises him, through his headset, to "descend right" while simultaneously advising the other plane to "climb left."

Contrast that robust quantity and immediacy of information with the information resources available to a schoolteacher—the pilot of a classroom, if you will. Until just recently, most schoolteachers got reliable information about the progress of their children *after* they no longer taught them. And until just recently, in most states, teachers had no objective, outside, reliable information on the progress of their children until their third or fourth year in school. For example, until recently most statewide student assessments were administered for a limited number of grades, with test results delivered to schools four to six months *after* a student had left the teacher who had supervised his or her work. It is as if a pilot received a report on his plane's airspeed and altitude several hours after a flight. How helpful would that be? Prodded by the new federal No Child Left Behind law, which requires annual testing, states are moving toward more real-time information about the progress of children. But it is fair to say that the education industry is a full twenty years behind other categories in the amount, immediacy, and usability of data.

R&D is the road to higher quality. It is also about getting more bang for the buck. As a primer on this topic, think about what has happened to the relationship between value and cost in the computer industry over the past decade. I can still remember my first laptop. It weighed in at well over 10 pounds, required its own carrying case because it would not fit into my briefcase, and had minuscule memory and an incredibly slow processor. It also cost over $3,000. Today, you can get more memory and speed than you could possibly use, a vast improvement in weight and size, and a significant *reduction* in price. Why? Continuous research and development, an industrywide belief that more value *can* be delivered for a lower price, and a sense of urgency that you had better get there before your competitor does.

Now let's look at what we have seen in the value-to-cost relationship of our schools. The following chart shows the percentage of children scoring at "below basic" on the NAEP over the past eleven years. Again, "below basic" is a level of performance bordering on illiteracy.

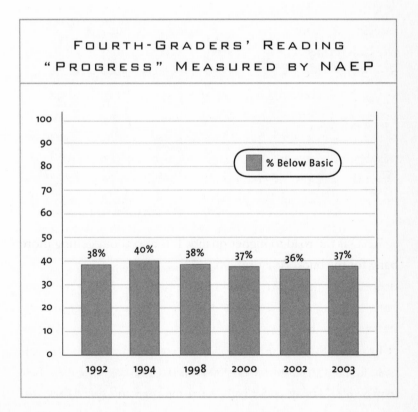

FOURTH-GRADERS' READING "PROGRESS" MEASURED BY NAEP

% Below Basic

	1992	1994	1998	2000	2002	2003
% Below Basic	38%	40%	38%	37%	36%	37%

What we see is that the percentage of fourth-graders with below basic reading skills is virtually the same in 2003 as in 1992—
no improvement. Now look at the following chart on how much
we have spent to educate, so to speak, each of these children:

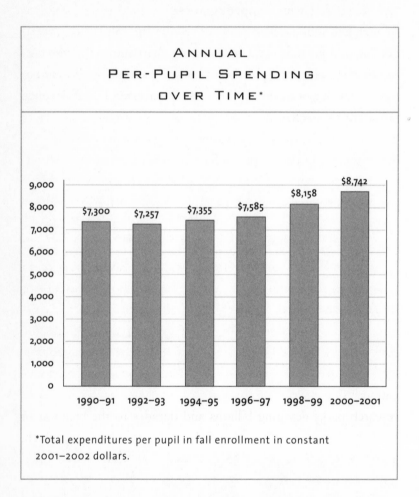

ANNUAL
PER-PUPIL SPENDING
OVER TIME*

*Total expenditures per pupil in fall enrollment in constant
2001–2002 dollars.

In the 1990–91 school year, we were spending $7,300 for each
child *we failed to educate.* In the 2000–2001 school year, we were failing them at a cost of $8,742. What we spent on failure had in-
creased by almost 20 percent in just a decade. Why? If we don't

provide our schools with R&D designed to crack the code of this problem, we are reciting a mantra well known in educational circles: Throw money at the problem and maybe that will fix it. This formula has become so ingrained in America's educational psyche that two false premises have been loaded onto the hard drives of many: (1) educational quality can only go up if spending increases, and (2) if spending decreases, then so must quality. Let me say right here: I'm for increased funding of our schools, something I will advocate later in this book. Invested in R&D-based system improvements and in higher teacher compensation, more dollars will make real differences and will represent a positive shift in our societal priorities. But billions of dollars are spent on funding initiatives that have not generated results—and those dollars should be the first source of funds for more worthwhile endeavors. I'm not a believer that anyone suggesting improved cost effectiveness should be greeted as a blasphemer.

Another way to compare and contrast the R&D going on in the private sector with that occurring in our schools is to look at the physical research-and-development facilities of other categories. Does K–12 education have anything approaching the equivalent of GM or Ford test tracks? Is there anything equivalent to the Bell Labs that drove such innovation in telecommunications? Our major pharmaceutical companies have built entire research parks devoting billions and decades to the creation of new drugs. Where are the parallels to this in education, which, again, is the second-largest sector of the American economy, behind only health care?

The creation of Edison Schools in the early 1990s is an instructive event. Prior to the launch of our first schools, we raised $45 million to do R&D on our school design. *It was, and still is, the largest school-design effort in U.S. K–12 education.* We recruited fifty talented people, divided them into design teams, and asked them to create competing school designs. We gave them a couple of years to do their work. The whole enterprise was viewed with amazement by many educators. Many saw it as incredibly lavish. Why do you need such an enormous amount of money to design a school? we were asked. Is there really anything to discover?

By modern business standards, I knew, the level of work we were doing was primitive. To help people understand that, I introduced into my stump speech of the day a chart contrasting the design of the Boeing 777 with that of the first Edison school. I'll introduce it to you today the way I did with audiences then, in the form of a pop quiz. I would put on the screen the following chart:

A DESIGN COMPARISON		
	1991–95 EDISON DESIGN	BOEING 777 DESIGN
■ Staff	50	
■ Design teams	4	
■ Budget	$45 million	
■ Culture	1 year	

I would ask the audience, "How many people were employed, full-time, to design the Boeing 777?" Answer: 10,000, compared with Edison's tiny 50. There would be a gasp from the audience. "How many design teams were there?" Answer: over 200, compared with Edison's 4. "What's a design team?" Answer: a group of 25 to 50 people working *on just one aspect of the plane.* For example, three teams worked on the layout of the cockpit. I'd then ask, almost always to widespread laughter, How many people designed our teachers' desks, the cockpit of a classroom? "What was Boeing's total design budget?" Answer: $3 billion, or about 70 times Edison's (which, again, was the largest design effort in U.S. education). And finally, I would point out that Boeing was a highly developed culture that had been doing this for eighty years, building on design after design, not some start-up, à la Edison, beginning with little or no on-board intellectual capital. The point: We have never as a nation applied anything like this kind of energy, resources, and effort to the design of our schools and the systems that support them.

One area of schooling, however, is considerably less fragmented: unions. Though the National Education Association (NEA) and the American Federation of Teachers (AFT) have local units generally side by side with school districts, they are tied together by strong state and even stronger national organizations. A visit to the NEA headquarters in Washington, which occupies a square city block, with a national staff of over 500, makes the point, particularly when compared, for example, with the National School Boards Association's headquarters, which has a staff of 130.

The flow of dollars is instructive as well. While the federal Department of Education and states send money to school districts, the reverse is true with unions: local union members send money, and lots of it, to both their state and national organizations. For example, if a teacher pays $500 in union dues, probably $150 goes to the national organization and $100 to the state organization. If you multiply just the national portion, $150, by the number of members of the NEA and AFT, you come up with hundreds of millions of dollars of infrastructure, systems, and firepower at the national level.

Contrast that with the entire budget of an average school district ($28 million). In a political or bargaining fight, who do you think is going to win? National full-time power against part-time local militia. I've always thought that the best-prepared teams on the field in education are the unions—and their success in getting what they want is one indication of it. They figured out that national scale matters.

A field trip to a school-district headquarters is informative in illustrating the issues of fragmentation. I chose Monroe County, Tennessee, for a virtual visit. It is a typical school district in an average-spending state. It has 5,000 students, eleven schools, and a budget of $29 million. The district headquarters is a few thousand square feet. (The combined design team for the Boeing 777 project had its "joint meetings" in a 7-million-square-foot hangar.) The district IT staff consists of three full-time people who are responsible for making sure all district technology systems function. (Federal Express's IT department has thousands.) And perhaps most important, the district has two people who are responsible for all levels of curriculum, from kindergarten reading to AP physics. They are the "content experts" within the district, the individuals responsible for everything that is taught. Time Inc., the world's largest magazine publisher, an entity that also has to have "content experts" in every subject area, has thousands of editors and writers working for its publications. These parallels are not perfect. Since American public schooling has no truly robust national organizations, it is impossible to make direct comparisons. These examples simply illustrate the great "resource chasms" that exist between robust national entities and local ones. Nor is this a criticism of the small districts of America. They are, for the most part, playing the hands they have been dealt and playing them as well as they can. But if we and they had a choice today, the question is this: Would we organize our school systems in this manner to achieve the greatest results?

By now, in the flow of this argument, some readers probably are wondering about those school systems that have achieved significant scale. Don't we have illustrations of the effect of scale in these few systems?

First, only three of the roughly 15,000 school systems in America, if you thought of them as businesses, would rank, on the basis of scale, as Fortune 500 companies, and they would be a long way from the top of the chart. The public schools of New York, Los Angeles, and Chicago would rank as #178, #323, and #481 on the Fortune list. That doesn't put them anywhere near the league of major category leaders such as GE, GM, Boeing, Merck, Time Warner, and Microsoft. Still, although not in what was once known as the "nifty 50" of corporate America, these three school systems are not mom-and-pop enterprises either. So should we not begin to see, from them, the kind of R&D, design, and sophisticated system buildup that you might find in similar-sized businesses?

The answer is yes, we should, but unfortunately, we don't. Not even close. Major U.S. corporations, depending on the category, invest 2 to 10 percent of their revenues in R&D. This means that even on the low side, New York City would be investing $250 million in R&D annually. If you were to call New York City Schools Chancellor Joel Klein to confirm the district's R&D spending, you would find that amount closer to zero. The average U.S. corporation spends between 2 and 3 percent of its revenues on training. Using the middle of that range, New York City should be spending $250 million per year on staff development. The actual number is nowhere near that.

What we clearly see is that achieving scale does not *ensure* that it will be used to advantage. Why? Because in the absence of an R&D-based system that drives the flow of dollars, the moneys that are available tend to be driven more by politics than by performance. Someone once called a particular board of education the Board of Employment, indicating that its real interests were jobs and adults, not education. The adult agenda, and more specifically, *the adult agenda of jobs,* controls many school systems, particularly large urban ones. R&D, technology, data systems, and even training are often seen as job-threatening. A well-supported, highly trained, and well-compensated teacher might not need two aides or might actually be able to teach more children, resulting in fewer teachers. And poor data systems almost invariably lead to buildings of clerks trying to make sense of it all.

Those are just some of the factors beyond scale and fragmentation that are standing in the way of schools that serve all our children. The next chapter examines other important ones.

CHAPTER 3

The Reefs
of Reform

My realization of the immense and severely limiting fragmentation of schooling initially led me to become involved in education reform. But as I engaged, I came to learn that
fragmentation was only one of the barriers to improvement that
school reformers face. Even now, I still discover new barriers to
positive change. Here are just a few.

On Your Mark, Get Set, You're Fired

Although many CEOs of New York's largest companies regularly
serve for one or two decades, the city's school system does not enjoy a similar continuity of leadership. In the past fifteen years, our
nation's largest school system has had six chancellors, the average
lasting two and a half years. Joel Klein, the current chancellor, arrived in February 2002, fresh with both the support of New

York's newly elected mayor and significant new powers to manage the city's schools. Klein's appearance on the scene was met with positive anticipation, as it should have been. He is a man of formidable intellect, great energy, and considerable accomplishment. If anyone can move New York's schools forward, it could well be Klein.

So began a pattern of events we'll call "the arrival of a new leader," a dance well known to, and perfected by, the old hands of education in New York as well as in other cities across the country. It is a ritual Klein was sure to have known about, having done his homework on this new world he was entering. And I am sure it is a rite Klein is convinced he will defeat, indeed has to defeat, if he is to achieve here the success he has grown accustomed to elsewhere.

I hope he is successful. The children of New York City deserve it, as does Klein. But if history is truly a guide, Klein and many of his colleagues nationwide have a difficult road ahead.

The comings and goings of school-system leadership in America, particularly in our larger, politically intense, media-rich cities, have become a highly ritualized—and unfortunately, eminently predictable—affair. It is as if someone had once published and distributed an underground outline of a play called *For Whom the School Bell Tolls,* containing the broad themes of this drama. It is a production for use almost anywhere, with not only a script for the lead actors and supporting players but complete instructions for the audience and the media as well.

The script allows for local adaptation, but its structure is as strict as that of a haiku or sonnet. Any production of the play must include six mandatory elements: the grand entrance; the promise of peace; encouraging signs; the small slips; the great crisis; and the denouement. Here's a brief description of each:

1. The new leader's grand entrance must be filled with promise and promises. The primary message is that finally an educational messiah has arrived who can fix our schools. If the new leader is wisely modest in the statement of his or her expectations, as most are, the press is required to inflate them, a precondition to later stages of the drama.

2. The new leader and the union head must praise each other, onstage. Each must express his or her openness toward the other, and public signs of a new, open dialogue must exist for at least six months.

3. Within a few months of the new leader's arrival, there must be at least a couple of anecdotal examples of progress. These must be hailed by the media; it is preferred that at least one be done in cooperation with the union; and no example of progress need be particularly significant. The audience must applaud loudly at this point.

4. Then come the small slips, two will do, missteps indicating that the new leader may not be infallible or omniscient. The press is required to be restrained—just questioning, not calling, yet, for the leader's head. The union must act with similar moderation, expressing "concern." The broader audience begins to become restless, talking during the play.

5. At this point, which is generally about eighteen months following the leader's arrival and some twelve months before his departure, a great crisis must occur. Productions adhering closely to the art form choose themes that have little to do with student learning, such as the distribution of condoms; sex education; social promotion; school closures; creationism; multiculturalism; unguarded public comments; or garden-variety scandals, which need not be directly related to the leader, though the closer the better. (One archetypal production in

Dallas sends the new leader to federal prison after the purchase of a bedroom suite for her home with school funds.) The media begin to pillory our protagonist for his or her shortcomings. An excellent irony is added if the failed expectations are of the media's own creation. It is expressly prohibited, however, for anyone to say that the great crisis has anything to do with the actual achievement, or lack thereof, of students.

6. Aside from the fact that the leader must go, the denouement allows great flexibility in the form of exit. The method and length of the execution are highly varied. At the very end, however, there is a final mandatory element: all parties must express their confidence that a new and better leader can be found. No one is allowed to criticize the art form itself. The stage is now set for a repeat of this highly entertaining tradition.

The highest praise is reserved for productions where no more than thirty months elapse between the accolade-filled arrival and the disgraceful departure of the leader. Dramas that extend beyond forty-eight months are highly discouraged. And there is one other unusual restriction: the fate of children cannot be significantly affected by the play. To adapt an old saying, the best productions believe children should be neither seen nor heard.

Some may find this a cynical view of what happens to the new leaders of school systems. If only that were true. Others, particularly those who have been around long enough to witness this acted out more times than Andrew Lloyd Webber's longest-running musical, will recognize it as a realistic portrayal of what too often happens to those who try to lead, and particularly those who try to change, big school systems today. In the nation's ten largest school systems over the past two decades, the average tenure for leaders is 3.7 years. That compares with 7.6 years as the average tenure over the past twenty years for the nation's top ten corporations. Said another way: the "leadership continuity factor" of America's top ten companies is 2 times better than that of its top ten school systems.

But let's go deeper. In districts where the problems are greatest, continuity is even worse. Here's a chart showing three particularly tumultuous districts:

DISTRICT TURNOVER WOES		
CITY	NUMBER OF LEADERS IN THE PAST 20 YEARS	AVERAGE TENURE, IN YEARS
Kansas City, Mo.	14	1.4
Washington, D.C.	9	2.2
New York City	8	2.5

Now contrast this with some of our best-performing companies, the ones we admire most:

CORPORATE LEADERSHIP CONTINUITY		
COMPANY	NUMBER OF LEADERS IN THE PAST 20 YEARS	AVERAGE TENURE, IN YEARS
General Electric	2	11
Federal Express	1	35
Microsoft	1	30
Dell	1	21

This kind of multiple-decade tenure is almost never seen in American education today. But it wasn't always so. On a visit to the Seattle school system some years ago, I was impressed by the photos of past superintendents on the waiting-room wall. Better than any chart, it told the story—as do the "photo walls" of many districts. In the early 1900s, leadership tenure was fifteen, twenty, twenty-five years. By the 1960s it was often down to five to seven years, and by the 1990s microtenures were the norm.

While reformers complain loudly when teachers are fired, we have largely ignored the round-the-clock firing squads taking aim at our school-system leadership. The effect on our schools cannot be underestimated. Every few years a new leader arrives—generally not from within the organization, because "if things are so bad, why would we promote someone from within?" The new leader brings a new plan, a new strategy, and new sayings. He or she often begins with an "out with the old" housecleaning, in terms of both top personnel and programs. (A new leader often brings his or her team from a previous district.) The old-timers within a system, those who have been through five or six leaders during their career, keep their heads down, go about their day-to-day activities more or less as in the past, and say, quite correctly, "This too shall pass." Soon enough it does. The new leader is fired, and the process begins again. Some of his or her programs survive, some don't, and programmatically, the design of the schools begins to look like an archaeological dig, with sediments from different rulers layered one unrelated type upon another.

It is important to note that very little can be accomplished during these short tenures—and what *is* accomplished is too often quickly undone by the next player in the chair.

As noted earlier, the fact that few leaders of our major school systems come from within compounds the problem. For example, the last six chancellors of the New York City schools were all recruited from outside the system. This means that the first year—which, in the case of New York City, represents 40 percent of the typical tenure—is largely spent finding one's way around, determining who is capable, and replacing those who are not (and making political-capital-consuming enemies in doing so). Perhaps during that first year one can unveil a "platform," but there is typically no time to get it executed. The second year a leader begins to execute his or her vision, but no one acquainted with school systems would tell you that one hundred years of "doing it our way" is overcome in anything close to one year. And then, all too often, in the third year the leader is gone.

To put this in some context, look at Edison Schools as a public school system. It would rank as the forty-seventh-largest in the United States, between Brevard County, Florida (#46), and Fulton County, Georgia (#48)—and I would be one of the longest-serving leaders of any system that large. I formally began Edison in 1991 and have now dedicated fourteen years to making it work. It is clear to me that I need to spend another fifteen years to achieve many of the things I want to do. Why would we believe the problems that took fifty or a hundred years to develop could be, presto, corrected in the short time we typically give our school-system leaders?

Bottom line: We have set up a system that deals the leaders of our public school systems almost impossible hands.

What factors cause this high turnover of our leadership? That's an easy one. Our schools are run, one way or another, by elected officials, generally in the form of school boards and mayors. Like the superintendents they supervise, these individuals themselves often have short-term tenures. Mayors last four to eight years. School-board members generally have four-year terms, and more important, a board majority can last only two years, since board elections are typically staggered. And that does not take into account the shifting sands that all political leaders stand on. Many boards have four-three-type majorities, and the changing of just one board member's mind can lead to changes in leadership and policy. These members have constituents to "feed," and all too often the soup du jour is seasoned with the head of the school system. Net, our schools are political institutions subject to the whims and the ebbs and flows of politics. Throw in that school-board meetings are often the best free theater in town, and then add that the media love, and even stoke, a good fight. Is it any wonder that school-system leadership lasts no longer than it does?

Muskets in a Nuclear Age

The Gallipoli-like rate at which we mow down school-system leadership is only one factor standing in the way of schools' dealing with the enormous quality issues presented in Chapter 1. Indirectly, it contributes to another. If a school-district leader knows he or she is likely to last only a few years, then, consciously or not, the size and importance of his or her "platform" are affected. In the context of what may be only a three-year tenure, a five-year project is viewed as very long-term, and a ten-year one is a hopeless dream. This leads to one of the first things I spotted when I began attending educational conferences years ago: a litany of often good but ultimately partial ideas that address only aspects of the whole and lack the comprehensiveness required to change our schools in a substantial way.

This is not a criticism of school-system leadership. Leaders are realistically responding to the terrain we have created. Knowing they have limited time, they pick a topic or two and tackle those as best they can. It may be principal recruitment, or middle schools, or reading programs, or early education, or technology, or professional development of teachers. While all of these are important, they are simply parts of the very large puzzle of schools and the systems that support them.

If there were a logical and rational hand-off to the next administration, perhaps this piece-by-piece approach would result in major steps forward. Unfortunately, that is not what happens. Indeed, a new leader, sensing that the programs (and participants) of the just-departed regime may well be politically radioactive, often distances himself or herself from the past, jettisoning programs and people that have just been put in place. (One of the great risks of attempting to do business in education is "regime change.") The result is a patchwork of incomplete and poorly integrated programs. The Brooklyn Bridge took thirteen years to build, led by the vision and execution of one man and his son. If that effort had been run as we run our school systems today, the waterfront of Lower Manhattan might now be a "museum of beginnings," a collection of the beginnings of ten bridges, each reaching partly across the river but none making it to the other side.

It's Only a Law

The regulations and policies governing our schools suffer the same fate as our leaders: a brief tenure.

Once, I was working on an important piece of state legislation with the speaker of a particular statehouse. It was late one night, and we were tired and a bit frustrated. He said to me, "Don't worry. It's only a law." Being a neophyte in the political process, I was a bit startled, thinking laws were things of great meaning and permanence. What he was saying to me was, "Kid, this might make some good headlines tomorrow and then last for just a little while." Knowing what I know now, I can see that he would have been even more accurate if he had said, "It's only an education law," for those suffer the fate he was describing with even greater frequency.

As superintendents come and go, so do the laws that govern schools. This or that state or federal administration comes up with a plan, gets the legislature to adopt it, and begins its execution. The next administration works to get it revoked or altered in favor of a different plan, and the process continues again and again.

The result: Just as the rank and file within schools view leaders as transient, they (and their leaders) view education laws the same way. Again, keep your head down and do your work, and the law or regulation will change soon enough.

The reaction of many within the education sector to No Child Left Behind, the Bush administration's seminal education policy, is instructive. (Full disclosure: While aspects of NCLB need refinement, I am an unabashed supporter of its overall thrust.) NCLB legislates that all schools must achieve a certain "gain rate" on their state exams every year. Specifically, by 2014, every school in the country must have all its children proficient in reading and math on state exams, and each school must progress toward that goal at a specified rate. If schools fail to achieve adequate yearly progress (AYP), there are consequences for every year that they continue to "fail." The consequences increase with every year of failure; the most significant consequences come after the fifth year of failure.

So how do many people react to this? First, most assume that tens of thousands of schools will ultimately fail the measures. That presumption appears not to be too far off the mark, as just a couple of years into the legislation's life, thousands of schools are in some sort of failure. It is anticipated that this list will grow every year. What happens if *virtually everyone* is breaking the law? It is a lot like having every car on an interstate traveling at 70 when the speed limit is 55. It becomes, if you will, an "optional law." In a worst-case scenario, it is like speed limits in Italy: they mean very little.

In the case of NCLB, an almost universal view is that there will be some sort of NCLB amnesty—when a very high percentage of schools are deemed failing, the law will simply be changed. As the saying goes, "When all else fails, lower your standards." In this case, the saying would read, "When everyone fails, it is okay." I doubt this amnesty will occur within the Bush administration, as it originated the bill, but it is a great likelihood in the next. Further, since NCLB is largely constructed so that it is interpreted by the states, there will be statewide "amnesties" at increasing rates. One reason is that no state wants a high percentage of its schools to be in a failing status.

The net result is this: Education reform laws such as NCLB are critical drivers of educational improvement, but their ability to drive that change depends directly on the education community's perception that the government won't blink when change actually is necessary. Unfortunately, history indicates it will.

Gifts That Can't Keep On Giving

Over the years, many well-intentioned observers have seen the poor performance of many schools and its deleterious effect on the fate of a large number of children and have asked, "What can we do?" One of their responses has been philanthropy.

I distinctly remember waking up one morning in December 1993 and reading on the front page of *The New York Times* that Walter Annenberg had made the largest gift in history to public schools, a grant of half a billion dollars. I had two thoughts in quick succession. The first: "Damn it, why didn't I get to him first!" The second: "Does Walter know that those funds will not last until lunch?" (At that time, public education was spending roughly $225 million *per school hour*!)

Philanthropy plays an important role in K–12. And it should play even more of a role. But like laws and leaders, philanthropy has distinct limitations—and even some dangers.

On the limitation front, the key one is scale. Foundations give an estimated $1.2 billion a year to public schools. As in 1993, such gifts do not go a long way. Our public schools, now a $400 billion enterprise, spend the entire amount in less than a school day. School districts blow through philanthropic funds so quickly, it's almost the same as running through leaders or laws. Philanthropic programs can easily become "here today, gone tomorrow," because the funds simply don't last. (A suggestion for givers is to focus relentlessly on finding pieces of the education puzzle where a gift can have a long-term, sustainable effect. Example: a $100 million gift related *only* to principal leadership development could well fund a twenty-year effort in that arena. In this regard, the California-based Broad Foundation has done a superb job focusing its resources on system leadership.) In a teacher union office, I once saw a poster that said, "Does the Pentagon Do Bake Sales?" What they were saying was true: philanthropy cannot be an answer to the gigantic operating issues of American education. The most it can do, at current rates of giving, is to provide important seed capital in critical qualitative arenas.

And the rhetoric of philanthropy can be counterproductive. In the past decade particularly, some philanthropies have been pushed to take sides (or have been used) in the debate over whether for-profits should be involved in public education. Seeing that it pleases some within the educational establishment, they have allowed themselves to be positioned as the "good guys" of the reform industry, intentionally or not painting "for-profit" reform entities in the reverse light. As many of these groups are funded by what *The New York Times* dubbed "Gulfstream liberals," it is an odd development. These same individuals and organizations made their money, more often than not, from founding large-scale for-profit organizations. They know all too well the benefits these companies bring to society—indeed, their foundations are a manifestation of that benefit. It is an unnecessary trap that the well-intentioned can be sucked into, often by opponents of change who would like nothing better than to create schisms between reform entities. The self-evident truth is that public educators need all the help they can get, including access to both philanthropists and the for-profit sector. There is plenty of room and work for both. Indeed, collaboration between the two should be the rule instead of some fabricated ideological divide—a civil war that delights those whose goal is simply to preserve the status quo.

Return to the One-Room Schoolhouse

About fifteen years ago, school reformers in both the United States and Britain became so frustrated with their inability to move school systems forward that they came forth with a new idea: What if we just did away with systems altogether? What if some existing schools "seceded" from their unions? What if we began new schools completely separate and apart from any systems? Could not individual "educational entrepreneurs" do a better job than what many considered oppressive, nonresponsive bureaucracies sapping our schools of funds and strength?

And so charter schools were born in America (as were their counterparts in Britain). Today over 3,300 charter schools serve nearly 800,000 students, approaching 2 percent of U.S. students. And there are cities where that penetration is much deeper. In Washington, D.C., for instance, nearly 15 percent of all public school students attend charter schools. Not only is D.C. our nation's capital, it is the charter capital of the United States. Some within the District believe that within the next decade, *half* the students there will be educated in charter schools.

Debate rages over whether charter schools are better or worse than the traditional public schools they are replacing and competing against. Dueling studies have been offered up by proponents and critics, with results showing that they do anywhere from substantially worse to substantially better. Readers of these studies should be cautious, taking into account the agendas of those conducting the research. In particular, readers should be wary of *any* study that looks *solely* at the current proficiency level of charter students. If a charter school has attracted very low-performing students and families who were desperate to escape low-performing public schools, those students invariably will *begin* at a very low point, a point well below "average" public schools in America—and even with dramatic improvement, it may take years for them to achieve average performance. Some charter opponents have attempted to position the information about these particular low-performing charter schools as an indicator of poor charter performance in general, shouting, "Charter-school students perform below averages!" This is akin to trumpeting as news the fact that patients who choose to see oncology specialists have a high rate of cancer. What observers should focus on instead is the *rate of gain*. How quickly is student performance rising in charter schools versus schools with *similar* demographics? That's what matters most. Definitive, long-term studies will be a while in coming, but I'll offer some predictions on what they will yield.

First, in cities with particularly dysfunctional school systems, charters will be the savior of tens of thousands of children, garnering enrollments approaching 50 percent.

Second, overall charter academic performance (as measured by student gain) is likely to be better than that of similar public schools. Not exponentially better, but enough to matter. Many factors will lead to this ultimate outcome. One you may find surprising: *The worst of charter schools will have their charters revoked,* a fate rarely suffered by their traditional public school counterparts. To say it another way, accountability will be stricter among charter schools, *resulting in the worst of them being removed from research samples.* Other factors that will lead to superior results are the focus of one board on one school—and the nearly zealot-like leadership that many charters are able to recruit, at least for a period of time. So overall, I believe charters will academically be a net positive.

But even if overall performance is higher, I think there will be less consistency within the category than its proponents would like, with a wide range of results, varying site by site from spectacular to disastrous. And I think year-to-year consistency of results at particular sites will vary widely as well. Sustainability will prove elusive, as charter boards struggle with replacing leaders who burn out. (This inconsistency, by the way, is also common in regular public schools.)

Finally, I think the crème de la crème of charter-school results will be in schools affiliated with robust charter systems and organizations, such as my company, Edison Schools, which provides systemic support to charter boards. While this is admittedly biased, it is both logically intuitive and supported by objective research.

On the intuitive side of the ledger, it just makes sense that schools within *good* systems are, in the long term, going to thrive more than those in isolation. Average units within great systems are going to outperform average units in a cottage industry. The support, experience, and expertise that systems bring to the table ultimately will tell. That is a fact supported by reality in virtually every other category in America. I see no reason it will be any different here.

It is also supported by considerable, if early, research on student achievement in schools managed by Edison Schools, the nation's largest charter-school operator. We have compared and contrasted results through our own assessment department and, more important to readers of this book, through commissioning a long-term study by the RAND Corporation, one of the nation's most respected social science organizations. What RAND reported earlier this year is that over time students in the schools we manage are, indeed, achieving academic gains substantially better than students in peer public schools—that is, schools with similar demographics.

This is not surprising data to us. It is consistent with a study completed by the Brookings Institution in 2003 that showed that charter schools managed by educational management organizations (EMOs)—companies or nonprofits that manage multiple charter schools—are showing better results than charter schools operating independently.

Last, charter schools that are part of larger charter systems will have the advantage of scale. Scale is particularly helpful in overcoming the Achilles' heel of charter schools: real estate. One sizable charter school—say, a 600-student school—can cost $10 million, just to create a facility comparable to those of traditional public schools. A public school system can handle such financing easily enough (just do a bond). But for a start-up charter board, the task can be daunting, often impossible. Facility challenges continue to slow the growth of charter schools. The point:

Even within this most promising reform arena, scale and sustainability haunt.

The Overarching Need for
Scale and Sustainability

The analysis in this chapter is meant to be neither a complete survey of the reform landscape nor a condemnation of it. It is rather a sampling intended to show the central, intertwining challenges that all reforms face. In particular, I wanted to shine a light on the two challenges that seem to thwart virtually all improvement initiatives in American schools: sustainability and scale.

If I were forced to choose, sustainability is the more important of the two. Without continuity, a leader cannot make a difference, and a service or system or law cannot have impact. Cultures cannot develop depth, institutional memory, and refinement if there is constant upheaval of leaders and policies. Yet this is the precise reality we have created in our public education system. As a nation, we must resolve to bring constancy and consistency to our schools and the systems that surround them. It is one thing for school boards to change with some frequency to reflect the will of the people. It is another for the "means of delivery" to be in constant turmoil. If we allow our school systems to be as unstable as banana republics, why should we expect our schools to be better than banana republic schools? Sustainability must become a watchword for anyone looking to make a difference in American education.

Next in importance comes scale. Think, for a moment, about the meaning of a Fortune 500 company "adopting" one school. In and of itself, it is surely not a bad thing. It helps the school—

and everyone at the company feels good about it. And if every Fortune 500 company "adopted" a school (and continued to do so for decades), well, then, there're 500 schools, and that's even better. *But there are over 90,000 public schools.* If we are going to take American schools to another level, we must think not only in terms of sustainable "fixes," but also in terms of changes that can achieve great scale, even if that scaling up takes thirty years. Education will not be improved through "cute" or "nice" efforts. It will be improved through sweeping, large-scale, systemic, and systematic changes. Our vision and our practical solutions have to be up to that task—a picture that Part III of this book attempts to paint.

PART II

A Path to Perspective

CHAPTER 4

My Very Public Education

I n 1988, I was forty-one and looking for a new frontier. I was restless, even though I was sitting nicely enough in my own little corner of the world.

For nearly twenty years I had been building a media company, Whittle Communications. It had become everything I could have wanted: successful, creative, rewarding, and filled with talented people. But as interesting and fun as the company had been, my passion for media seemed to be waning.

So I was looking. And not just for any frontier. I wanted one, like politics or journalism, that mattered—something that might make our nation better—and that would use and test and stretch the skills I had honed.

My search might have been quixotic (others will judge that), but it certainly was not casual. It was actually funded and staffed. I assembled a small team, and we spent periodic retreats looking for important, unexplored (or underexplored) ideas. But as intentional as our effort was and as ready as we were, the discovery itself—as so often is the case—was, in the end, an accident. And at the intersection of that accident was something called Channel One.

Channel One, America's first truly national news program for teenagers, was piloted by Whittle Communications in 1989 and launched nationally in 1990. Like so many things the company did, Channel One broke the tethers of conventional wisdom. It had several (then) radical premises: (1) Daily news for children within a school could enhance the educational process. (Example: News of a shuttle launch might lift off a science lesson later that day.) (2) Left to their own devices, teenagers would probably not leave MTV for CNN, nor would they enthusiastically embrace "adult" news even if it was forced upon them. Therefore, news content should be tailored to a teenage audience and be a required part of a school's curriculum. (3) Simply producing the program would not be enough. The delivery system itself would have to be built from the ground up. Few schools at that time had a way to receive a TV signal and then distribute it, simultaneously, to every classroom. (4) Somehow we would have to do all this "for free." At that time, we could think of no way schools could afford the roughly $200 million tab required to build the required technological pipeline, much less the cost of producing a daily news program with substantial international content. That "somehow" turned out to be two minutes of advertising each day in our twelve-minute news broadcast.

So we launched Channel One, and in doing so I was introduced to American education—and it was introduced to me. There have been smoother meetings.

Channel One was extraordinary on many levels. In just thirty-six months from its national launch, 40 percent of all middle schools and high schools in the United States adopted the program. By 1993, 8 million teenagers were watching Channel One *every* school-day morning, nearly 100 times those watching CNN on a daily basis. No other news program could claim that daily reach. Young reporters from Channel One were dispatched around America and the globe to produce stories edited specially for teenagers. (A few, such as Anderson Cooper, now of CNN, learned so much they ultimately were snatched up by national networks.) It was a somewhat mind-bending operational achievement. In a time when satellite dishes were still several feet across, we placed them on the tops of 12,000 school buildings, we installed 300,000 TVs in classrooms in those schools, and we laid 5,000 miles of cable *within* these school buildings to tie it all together. Students liked the program, and so did journalists. It received, just three years after its launch, one of the highest accolades in television journalism, the Peabody Award, for a special feature on AIDS. And it was good business, too. Channel One revenue went from zero to $80 million in three years, and it was generating $30 million a year in operating margin, every bit of which was needed to repay the initial $200 million capital investment.

It was also controversial. *Very* controversial. Debate raged in educational circles over the appropriateness of allowing advertising in America's classrooms. Opponents said it was a violation of the sanctity of the educational environment. Supporters said the advertising was benign and well worth it, because it enabled educationally valuable news and desperately needed technology. For several years (and even to this day) the debate volleyed back and forth.

To "sell in" Channel One, representatives of the company attended an astounding 30,000 meetings with school boards. As chief spokesperson for Channel One, I was called to many. In addition, I attended dozens of educational conferences to discuss, debate, and, primarily, defend Channel One. During this "tour" two things happened that changed the course of my life. First, just as a candidate is shaped by a campaign as much as voters are, I began to see and learn about the terrain of public schools, far beyond the topic at hand. When you are last on the agenda of a school-board meeting, you see and hear a lot! Second, I was extended an invitation that forced me to synthesize what I was seeing. The Tennessee Business Roundtable asked me to share my thoughts, not about Channel One but about education itself. Specifically, the Roundtable asked me to address their group on "What Would You Recommend to Improve America's Schools?" I had six months to prepare. As I never take a speech casually, I began to think a great deal more about the question.

My preparations for that speech, given sixteen years ago in the fall of 1989, produced a key premise that became the genetic code of a new idea, a concept that would become an antidote for the "cottage industry" fragmentation described in Chapter 2. I proposed that America's schools would improve if they were organized in larger, national systems. I argued that our nation should build the first of what I hoped would be many national systems of schools in America. I postulated that this newfound scale, and the freedom it would bring from the constraints of tradition, would unleash powerful new forces in education, including completely unheard-of levels of investment in research and development. New school designs and new systems of support would emerge—and bring new levels of success.

I did not intend to implement this idea personally. Nor was I even wholly on the right track. In the original speech, I suggested that the federal government should take on the project, building the first such system of schools. It was not until later that I realized this approach would not work, that the best way to implement the idea was through large-scale, comprehensive, private-sector partnerships with local school districts. Not in the old, limited ways in which private companies traditionally had become involved—as vendors that drop texts or technology off at the classroom door, steering well clear of actual accountability for achievement. Instead, I came to the realization that this level of change could not happen without hip-deep private-sector integration in both the programmatic design and the full operation of schools.

While the idea was not complete, it was completely intriguing. It occurred to me that this was perhaps the frontier I had been seeking. Like so many others in the years to come, I was pulled into the gravity field of this powerful idea, never to escape. Soon I was not just talking about it. I was far out to sea, with land no longer in sight, working to make it happen.

Thus was born Edison Schools.

I did not know then what I know now: that to pursue this idea, I would flirt, multiple times, with financial ruin, both personal and corporate; that like Steven Jobs except without the public notice, I would be fired and then rehired by the company that I had created; that before we made our first dime, we would need to raise about $1 million per week, every week, for thirteen years, or about $675 million; that for some, this investment would turn out to be very profitable, while for others, very costly; that we (and particularly I) would be pilloried in the press, even vilified, for trying to build a business that would bring about better schools; or that this idea would demand, by the time I am probably forced to retire from this cause, thirty years of my life, and that even then, my initial vision will have been only partially realized. And I had not a clue that this idea would shape me even more than I shaped it.

I did not foresee how worlds beyond schools, particularly those of politics and capital markets, would move and evolve in ways to support this new concept. Politicians, looking to lead as well as pressured by constituents unhappy with their children's schools, would take the initial steps to break the monopoly of the old way, clearing, to some degree, the roads we would travel (though, we later would learn, simultaneously inciting some of the entrenched leaders of that old monopoly to attack and demonize us). I did not know that the computer and the Internet, two tools that would be central to future school designs, would drop in price and expand in capabilities to a point where they could become a much more important part of schools. And I did not foresee that the capital markets, in a way that might not exist again for some time, would be open to, and even look for, important, long-term ideas seeking major funding.

But for all that I did not know, I knew a lot. I sensed the significance of the concept. I knew we might change the way education is delivered in America, and that in doing so we could change, for the better, the futures of millions of children. I knew we could become, over time, one of America's most significant companies. I understood what a "share point" was, and that one share point—that is, 1 percent of American public education—equaled a Fortune 500 company. I also knew that I was perhaps uniquely qualified to lead this effort. It required a combination of skills I'd been told I had: recruiting a cast of resourceful people, creating a culture for innovative product design, raising money (more than I had ever imagined!), communicating a clear vision to diverse constituencies, taking heaps of criticism, and not breaking under pressure. My first twenty years of work might not have been my ultimate calling, but they were a terrific training ground for what lay ahead.

Believing Is Seeing

In 1989 the idea that a private company would manage a national network of public schools seemed outlandish and far-fetched.

Today, Edison touches and improves the lives of over 270,000 public school students. You can find schools where we work near London (with significant Muslim populations); just across the Mexican border in California (with just-arrived Spanish-speaking students); on the chilly shores of Lake Superior (in middle-class white neighborhoods); in the impoverished neighborhoods in the shadow of the Capitol in Washington, D.C. (with virtually 100 percent African-American enrollment). To do our work, we have had to learn the laws, the unique languages, and the Byzantine financial and operational realities of public education in different states and countries. Public education is a culture unto itself, with a language all its own. ISTEP, AYP, SAT-9, FCAT, NCLB, Safe Harbor, IEP, ELL, AMO, BOCES, RESAs, Title I, Title II, BSF—these are but a small sampling of the educational codes that now make up my daily life. I've never learned the native language of my wife (Italian), but I'm now reasonably fluent in Eduspeak.

For my work, it is a required fluency, and one I acquired with some considerable pain. While my career in public education began from the outside and from a perspective of 30,000 feet, my insights into its future have been tested, shaped, and honed by a decade and a half of total immersion in its waters—with moments close to drowning (from which some of my greatest lessons have come). I am not a detached theorist. I've burned rubber on the road of schools, been burned by getting too close to the sun, and, I seem to recall, been burned in effigy. While I would not necessarily wish to relive all those moments, they have been essential to the development of the ideas I propose in this book. I offer, below, a few of the more pivotal times and events in Edison's history.

These vignettes may have further usefulness to the reader. The practicality of the solutions proposed later in this book may not be self-evident. I hope the following stories will demonstrate that I am, in fact, very familiar with the realities of public education. To rephrase, the old saying "Seeing is believing" may have to be reversed here. You may need to believe in me a bit before you see what I see.

Start Big, For There Will Be Those Who Want to Bring You Down

Those people who know of Edison probably first heard of it following a story on the front page of *The New York Times* on May 26, 1992. The above-the-fold headline read "Yale President Quitting to Lead National Private-School System." If Benno Schmidt, the six-year president of one of the world's great universities, was prepared to give up lifetime tenure, prestige, and security, then something big must be afoot, the *Times* seemed to intuit. And it was.

From the day I first conceived Edison, I knew that its success would be determined in large part by the amount of initial "throw weight" it was able to coalesce. I knew that orbital speed would only be achieved with an initial Atlas-like boost. I sensed that the resistance was going to be tough and the journey long—and that the inertia gained through a powerful launch could see us through a great deal. Our accelerating mass could and would come from multiple ingredients, including financial capacity and excitement over the idea itself. But a particularly critical ingredient was going to be the assembly of an exceptional team, one that would in and of itself give credibility and gravity to the idea.

My first order of the day was to find a world-class educator to be my close partner in this endeavor and to serve as the recognizable, unimpeachable educational credibility of the company. I knew that as a media entrepreneur (especially one who had just absorbed a rather thorough public thrashing to successfully launch Channel One!), I would not be able to command any initial educational high ground. So off I went to find a partner. A bit of luck intervened to assist.

In the summer of 1991 there was a small dinner party in Sag Harbor, on Long Island, at the home of friends, Ed and Carol Victor. Ed is a successful literary agent (including for this book), and as is typical with him, the guest list was interesting. Among them were ABC anchorman Peter Jennings; the author of *Ragtime,* E. L. Doctorow; and, yes, the president of Yale, whom I had never met. I mentioned that I was planning to hatch a new idea called, at the time, the Edison Project. (One of my tried-and-true ways to develop ideas is simply to begin discussing them with anyone who will listen. I find concepts gain momentum that way.) To my surprise—and perhaps to the chagrin of my host—the dinner party turned into a heated debate. Everyone seemed to have a point of view. Doctorow simply hated the idea, saying something to the effect that it was a corruption of the whole concept of public education—that profit should not be a factor in the provision of a public service. I responded that if our public schools were to be purged of profit, then we would lose everything from the food in the cafeteria to the textbooks in our classrooms. That irrefutable logic just stoked his ire more. He summed up his argument by saying that my ability to persuade with logic made me an even more dangerous person.

On the drive home I didn't focus on Doctorow's negative reactions. Instead I wondered about my new acquaintance, Benno. I recall saying to my wife, Priscilla, that Benno seemed more open than most to the Edison concept.

So, within days, I called him in New Haven and asked if I might come to talk with him more about the Edison idea. He readily agreed. We met at Mory's, a Yale watering hole dating to 1861, and there I came straight to the point: "What would you think of leaving Yale, moving to Knoxville, Tennessee [where Whittle Communications and the beginnings of Edison were then based], and heading up the first effort to build a national system of schools?" Working from small notes next to my plate, I argued that his educational capital could be put to even greater use fixing the dire issues within our schools.

As you might suspect, he did not accept on the spot. In later speeches about the beginning of Edison, he said, only somewhat jokingly, that he was concerned that he was having lunch that day with a slightly deranged fellow! But it was the beginning of a year-long series of discussions that culminated in his becoming CEO of Edison, with my serving in the role of its chairman. When announced, it was a seminal, company-elevating event, and the American establishment recognized it as such. The media was smitten with the incongruity of it (Private Ivy League meets Public Elementary School), the first President Bush invited us for a small private lunch at the White House to hear what we were up to, and many governors followed suit. Fifteen years later and with rotated titles, Benno and I are still together. Edison would not be where it is—or be at all—were it not for his courage and contributions.

To many, Benno was Edison's first recruit. But in fact, during the year he and I were "courting," a very serious talent search was under way to assemble what we called the core team. We thought of them as the original seven educational astronauts. Tom Ingram, a senior executive at Whittle Communications who had earlier served as chief of staff for Tennessee governor Lamar Alexander, headed up the recruitment effort. Tom's assignment was to find seven highly regarded leaders from a variety of fields. The emphasis of the search was on creativity and an eclectic mix.

Experience in education was not mandatory. Working with Benno, the team would lead the development of the Edison school design. They would be given three years and an R&D budget of $45 million. The capital was being provided by Time Warner, Philips Electronics, and the Daily Mail and General Trust, one of Britain's largest publishers, along with, when the going got rough, some $30 million in personal guarantees from me. (All the initial investors were general partners in Whittle Communications, and it is interesting to note both the stature and international flavor of the board: Lord Rothermere, the chairman and owner of one of England's largest newspaper empires; Steve Tumminello, the U.S. CEO of Philips, based in Holland; and Gerald Levin, destined to be Time Warner's future CEO.)

The team came together in the spring of 1992, and its quality may well have been the deciding factor in Benno's joining the company. John Chubb, a Brookings/Princeton/Stanford scholar and a nationally known author on education (credited with popularizing the idea of school vouchers), was one of the first to sign up. I remember meeting at a hotel in D.C. where I said, "John, you've been writing about schools for some time. Now it is time to *make some*." (Along with Benno, John is still with the company today. He is Edison's chief education officer.) Checker Finn, a former undersecretary of education and a tough and always piercing critic of U.S. schools, was another high-profile addition. Lee Eisenberg, a former editor of *Esquire*, and Dominique Browning, assistant managing editor at *Newsweek*, brought the kind of creativity and aesthetic contribution I had often seen in my media days. Dan Biederman, well known in New York City as a leading proponent of public/private partnerships, like the rehabilitation of the Grand Central Terminal area, agreed to give us time. Nancy Hechinger came to us from Silicon Valley and Apple. She introduced the then revolutionary idea that every student should receive a computer free from schools, just like textbooks. Sylvia Peters also signed up. She was the only K–12 educator on the team, having distinguished herself as a terrific principal of an inner-city Chicago school. We were exceedingly selective, but every offer made was accepted—except one. Wendy Kopp, the founder of Teach For America, refused us, despite my repeated efforts to convince her otherwise. She wanted to follow through what she had just begun at TFA, and she has done that in a big way. (But in one of those twists of fate, Wendy's husband, Richard Barth, is now a key executive at Edison.)

So off we went. Public education had never seen anything like this group—and most of us had never seen anything like public education except from a student's perspective! This critical mass of talent (along with another forty researchers and designers they recruited) made up the nucleus of the Edison research effort. It might not have been the Manhattan Project (that's the origin of the "Project" part of the initial name), but their work propelled us for nearly a decade. Even Edison's die-hard opponents had to concede that the concepts underlying Edison's school design were best of breed and imaginatively integrated. At the end of the day, though, it was not just what they created that mattered. It was also the fact that no other effort like this had ever been attempted. Their work made a statement, not just by what they did, but also by raising an important question: If public education is as important as we all say it is, why on earth hadn't this been done before?

You Can Be Fired from a Job but Not from a Cause

A few years ago a professor informed me that he was writing a book on leadership in which I was being used as an example of "failed leadership." As you might imagine, that did not quite make my day. This was after some highly publicized difficulties Whittle Communications had experienced when I overextended the company by undertaking too many major initiatives at once. Edison was just one of four very significant *simultaneous* launches by the company. I had violated a rule that I knew very well: focus. My businesses had enjoyed twenty-five years of almost uninterrupted upward trajectory, and perhaps I had begun to believe up was the only direction we could go. I was wrong—and things went wrong. One of my least-favorite headlines of the time was on the cover of *The New Yorker*: "Whittle's Long Swan Dive." *Splat!*

Though I wasn't thrilled about the professor's suggested angle of attack, I agreed to talk to him nonetheless (being a longtime believer that an open-door policy with the press and academia may not yield wet kisses but will probably result in more balanced coverage than a stiff arm). As we talked, and for reasons I don't recall, I recounted a story to him that I had never publicly told. He found it fascinating, so much so, he said, that he was going to alter the direction of the chapter he had planned on me and use it as an example of a concept he called "Leadership Without Portfolio." Here it is in abbreviated form:

In 1994 and 1995, in the midst of the crisis at Whittle Communications, I was selling off or closing down divisions of the company in order to save certain other parts of it. It was Sophie's Choice on a corporate scale, and I had made my decision: I would focus on Edison, even though it was then only in its infancy. That is how I would spend the remainder of my career. Though I was deeply attached to Edison, its board of directors was growing less attached to me. They were increasingly concerned that the difficulties in other parts of my businesses could impair Edison's ability to raise cash for its expansion. The board asked me to take a back seat, both publicly and in the operation of the company, even though I was, at that moment, covering Edison's payroll out of my own pocket, would soon own or control 50 percent of its stock, and was committing to fund the bulk of its capital needs for the next couple of years. To spare the company and me embarrassment, it was dressed up a bit and resulted in no public hanging, but make no mistake about it: I had been fired. I still owned my shares, and that carried some veto capability. But I had no "affirmative" authority, no title, no compensation—and everyone in the company knew it.

I had a decision to make. What was I going to do? Should I just leave and begin again? For virtually every day since the middle of college, I had been an entrepreneur, a leader and builder of organizations. The idea of being a board member rather than a "field general" was alien to me. So I had a novel idea. Simply put, I decided to keep coming to work—as a volunteer in my own company. As Woody Allen says, "Eighty percent of success is just showing up." For two full years, I showed up every day and simply asked people around the company, "What can I do to help?" I was paid nothing, covered my own expenses, and had no authority to direct anyone to do anything (which, actually, wasn't that unusual, because I have never been an "authority-oriented" leader anyway). And within no time at all, my days were filled completely. It was a hugely productive period, actually. Within two years, the board asked me to return as CEO.

I learned that one can lead from anywhere on the field. And more important, I demonstrated to those around me, and to myself, how committed I was to the idea of Edison. That commitment has never wavered. A few years later, during another serious bump in the road, I was being interviewed by a journalistic team from PBS and *The New York Times* (John Merrow and Diana Henriques). The question was put, "What would you do if Edison failed?" With a lack of hesitation that surprised even me, I answered, "Do it again."

Good Grades Do Not Equal Good Politics

Over the past decade, Edison has expended roughly $2 billion. Of that, something on the order of $10 million, or only $1 million per year, was spent to communicate to various audiences what we do. By corporate marketing and government relations standards, that is a pittance. When you consider that during much of the decade the company was under steady and concerted attack from organizations that opposed private-sector involvement in schools, organizations with lobbying and communication budgets in the hundreds of millions, ours was a fraction of a pittance. And it was a fundamental error in our initial plan.

We began the Edison adventure believing that if we operated good schools, everything else would work itself out. In particular, we thought that the best communications strategy was a good product. We were immensely naïve. Running good schools was required, but it was far from sufficient.

As previously noted, the rate of increase in student achievement at public schools that partner with Edison surpasses the increase rate at peer schools—schools with similar demographics. How could that not be lauded in the press? How could our phone not ring off the hook with districts asking us to work for them, too?

The answer is simple enough, although it completely eluded us at the time. Student achievement was not viewed by many as a central element in either the operation of schools or their coverage by the media. Other than the annual printing of scores, not a lot of attention was really paid to student achievement. The number of people in school leadership positions who could not tell you, without reference material, the rate of achievement gain (or loss) of their students was (and is) shocking. The same was true of many reporters covering schools. While real progress has been made, this issue still exists to a considerable extent.

Too often, what rules schools is politics, not grades.

We learned that the hard way in Dallas. In 2000, over the objection of some school-board members, Edison was hired to manage seven of the district's lowest-performing schools. Just months after we began, Bill Rojas, the crusading superintendent who had brought us to town, was asked to leave, another victim of Fire the Superintendent Syndrome. Adhering to our belief that performance would trump politics, we kept our heads down and went about our work. Three years into our five-year contract, we got the same treatment as Rojas received: we were shown the door, despite the fact that our schools had outgained similar schools within the district (a fact we were never able to clearly communicate).

I used to believe that two bottom lines must be attended to in the world of education: academic (the most important, because without it nothing else matters) and financial. I now know that in the world of schools there are three realities, each of which must be managed to reach and sustain success: achievement, money, and politics. In the language of education, we are "advanced" at the first, approaching "proficient" at the second, and still "basic" in the third.

If All Politics Is Local, All Education Is More So—and It Should Stay That Way

My belief in the power of scale, and the good that scale can create for American education, is evident throughout this book. I first arrived at that view on a logical basis. It now has been reinforced by years of experience in the field. Perhaps, then, it may seem odd that I am equally a believer in local control of our public schools. To be candid, in the early days of Edison, I mouthed that view more out of practicality and political realities than profound belief. Now I can say in a heartfelt way that locally based *control* of schools, wed with national and global capabilities, is the right way to go, and for one great reason: it produces better results in the classroom. Edison's experience in Washington, D.C., is a case in point.

Donald Hense, Edison's partner and "boss" in D.C., is a man on a mission. Following graduation from Morehouse College and Stanford and stints as an administrator in higher education at Dartmouth and Boston College, he heads a community organization in D.C. called the Center for Youth and Family Development (and, before that, he led the oldest social-service entity in D.C., Friendship House). Beginning in 1998, Hense decided to devote substantial portions of his energy to creating new educational options for the children of D.C. He founded and is chairman of the board of the Friendship Charter School—the largest charter entity in D.C. and now the third-largest provider of K–12 education in D.C. overall (behind only the D.C. School District and the archdiocese). Friendship now educates about 3,000 students. And it does so extraordinarily well. In a community where only 30 percent of graduating students attend college, all but two members of Friendship's first graduating class went on to higher education! At the elemen-

tary and middle levels, in past years Friendship campuses have routinely posted some of the biggest gains on D.C.'s mandated exams.
Note the progress of Friendship-Edison's Chamberlain campus,
which serves nearly a thousand children, virtually all of whose families meet one of the federal definitions of poverty:

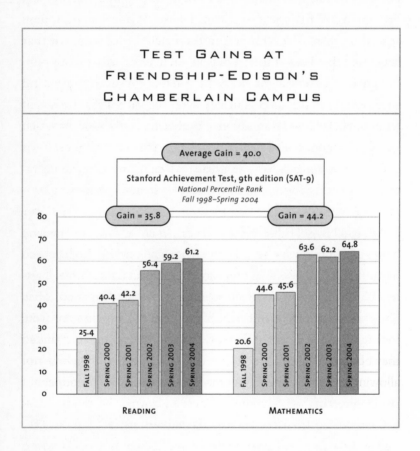

Students entering Chamberlain in the fall of 1998 were scoring
between the 20th and 25th percentiles on mathematics and reading on the SAT-9, scores that were an almost certain predictor of
their eventually dropping out of school. Six years later Chamber-

lain students, on average, scored above the 60th percentile—ensuring that virtually all students will graduate from high school and be ready for college, work, or other good options they would not enjoy if they dropped out. In six years Hense's vision and effort tripled the academic performance of these students and exponentially improved their life potential. And this is just the beginning. Over the next five years, Hense and Edison want these schools to reach the 80th percentile, which would place them at levels of achievement found only in a few D.C. public schools.

Donald Hense will graciously tell you that Edison has been, and is, important to the success of his schools. And I will tell you that without Hense and his significant local team, the schools in which we work would not be nearly as good as they are. The results in D.C. have taught me how powerful a local/national partnership can be. We provided our school design, systems, and training programs (and over $30 million in capital to help acquire the four campuses). And Hense and his team did things we could never have accomplished alone. Like pilot captains who guide ships into harbors they do not know, they navigated the intricate political waters of D.C. They found real estate we would have missed. They knew whom to hire (and fire). They spotted mistakes we were making that would have been less obvious to us—and demanded they be addressed. They continuously held our feet to the fire, not allowing us to be simply better than the school down the street but demanding that we become the best in town. The result: 3,000 D.C. students (and growing) have a brighter future.

Barbecue and Silver Linings in Philadelphia

Vanity Fair magazine once characterized me as "genetically upbeat." If inherited, I think it is from both my father and mother, who still maintain a spirit that inspires me. But in the spring and summer of 2002, even I was having difficulty finding a positive view.

For a year (that seemed like five), Edison had been struggling with a highly controversial situation in Philadelphia. As noted earlier in this book, former Pennsylvania governor Tom Ridge had decided to take control of the city's school district (the nation's eighth-largest) following years of anemic test scores and with a financial crisis looming. We were asked to play a leading role. The move sparked a huge political fight between the Republican administration in Harrisburg and the Democratic mayor of Philadelphia, John Street. There was intense local media coverage—literally hundreds of newspaper articles over the course of a year. The national press also was substantially engaged. And there was plenty of theater to engage them. Perhaps the most creative was Mayor Street's moving into the district's administration building with the pledge that he would have to be removed by force. There were serious protests in the streets. And Edison was at the fulcrum of the conflict—the football being kicked up and down the field.

Initially, the plan had been that Edison would manage 60 to 70 of the district's most challenged schools and play a leading role in the central office. The final outcome bore little resemblance to the blueprint. After a year of controversy, which, among other things, devastated Edison's stock, there would be no engagement with the overall district. As for our management of schools, we were asked to work with twenty schools—with an even greater number, twenty-five, being divided among six competitors, none of whom had been pummeled in the process of bringing this reform to Philadelphia. The assignment was the largest we had ever received, by a factor of three. When compared with our expectations, however, as well as those of Wall Street and the press, it was a bruising defeat—at least at the time.

Just as important, we were asked to engage with these twenty schools on a basis very different from our traditional model. With the exception of principal selection, we would have little or no role in personnel decisions, and we had no real authority over the school budget. We were being asked to turn around twenty of the country's most difficult schools with two critical levers removed from our approach. The district administration nicknamed it the "thin-management model" to contrast it with our customary approach, which gave us significant site authority. We considered declining the assignment, but given the enormous cost incurred (nearly $2 billion, or 95 percent, of our stock value gone, and our image battered), we saw no choice but to try, even with what we viewed as a highly compromised situation.

Barbecue was discovered, I've heard, when a barn burned down, pig enclosed. Whether that is true or not, the image is fitting enough—the idea that something good, even great, can come from a conflagration. It happened to us in Philadelphia. Three years after our nearly company-busting start there, it might well be that Philadelphia has accelerated in multiple ways the whole movement of private-sector engagement with public schools. I would never have imagined that in the summer of 2002.

In future history books on education, Philadelphia might be credited with three key contributions: (1) the first large-scale, simultaneous use of multiple competing outside education providers (already being called in education circles the "multiple-provider model"); (2) an unprecedented level of analysis of the effects of private-sector engagement; and (3) the introduction of a more politically acceptable method for private-sector involvement.

While dozens of school districts in the United States have engaged entities to manage schools or turn them around, those efforts have typically had two things in common. First, they have included a relatively small number of schools. For example, prior to Philadelphia, Edison's largest engagements were Dallas and Las Vegas, which each partnered with Edison to operate seven schools. Second, districts typically deployed only one provider. What Philadelphia did, admittedly through late-night political compromise versus thought-through design, was (1) contract far more schools than anyone else (45 schools, or around 20 percent of its entire system) and (2) deploy simultaneously seven different providers, not one.

The significance of this is beyond degree. It changed the *nature* of private-sector engagement. By moving to multiple providers, Philadelphia accentuated the *concept* of private-sector engagement—*not a specific company.* In Philadelphia, it was done from a defensive posture: to distance the administration and district from Edison, which had been made radioactive via the demagoguery of the opponents of the state takeover. In the future, however, school districts can *begin* with this strategy. It keeps the argument at the conceptual level (where it belongs) and lessens the ability of ideologues to undermine the initiative by demonizing a single pioneering company.

The scale of Philadelphia's effort led to the second benefit: a very different level of analysis. When a district uses private-sector help in a small number of its schools, it is easy to dismiss the effect (positive or negative) as idiosyncratic or flawed because of the small samples. Not so in Philadelphia. In this district one can compare and contrast, in large sample sizes, not only the differences between "provider schools" and "regular" district schools, but also the difference in results between providers, including an almost never used concept in schools: the relationship of cost to effect, or cost effectiveness.

Data is already flowing out of Philadelphia that will shape educational discussion and research for years to come. Most surprising to many (but not to me) is the fact that those schools not managed by external providers have been among the largest gainers over the past three years. *Fact: Schools run by the district itself experienced the highest achievement gains of any large urban district in the United States in the 2003–2004 school year.* Why, after years of insignificant gains, would that be? Could it be that competition does raise all boats? Could it be that every school leader in town said, perhaps quietly, "I'm not going to let those new private managers show me up. We're going to beat them!" And who wins this race? Could it be all the students of Philadelphia?

For a few examples of what Philadelphia is contributing to the educational community, let me show you three charts. The first is an eight-year history of the twenty schools Edison was assigned to manage.

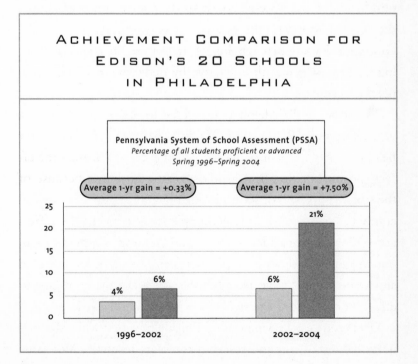

ACHIEVEMENT COMPARISON FOR
EDISON'S 20 SCHOOLS
IN PHILADELPHIA

Pennsylvania System of School Assessment (PSSA)
Percentage of all students proficient or advanced
Spring 1996–Spring 2004

Average 1-yr gain = +0.33%   Average 1-yr gain = +7.50%

1996–2002   4%   6%
2002–2004   6%   21%

In 1996, only 4 percent of the children in these schools were deemed "proficient" on Pennsylvania's state assessment. That changed by only 2 points in the six years between 1996 and 2002, an average rate of gain of 0.33 percent per year (that's *point* 33—a third of 1 percent!). Over the next two years, proficiency in these schools more than tripled, and the annual rate of gain increased from 0.33 percent to 7.5 percent per year—an increase of *over twentyfold.* If these changes had occurred in one or two schools, their statistical significance could be argued, or it might be asserted that the effects were isolated or unreplicable. But this was not a couple of schools. It was 7.5 percent of the schools in the eighth-largest system in America. It was not a couple of hundred children. It was 12,000. Suddenly, the numbers start to be undeniable.

And then look at the following chart:

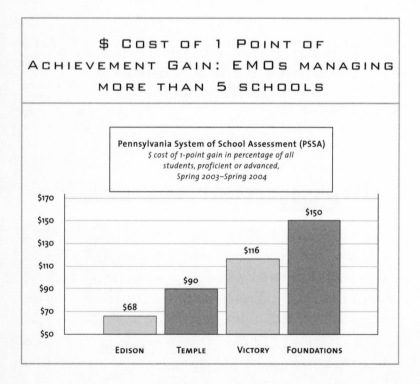

You are viewing a unique document, one that shows the gain of students on the basis of actual, not theoretical, costs. This takes the four largest providers in Philadelphia and measures the cost of each point of achievement gain they delivered in the 2003–2004 school year. It tells an interesting story. Though Edison, because of its proprietary model and systems, was paid nearly twice as much as other providers on a per-student basis, it actually delivered much higher gains—resulting in the best cost per point of gain. This chart is the equivalent of the introduction of "miles per gallon" in the automotive industry.

Finally, Philadelphia has shown that the public and private sector can engage on more flexible terms than initially imagined. As I said previously, we were extremely reluctant to agree to conditions that diminished our authority within the schools we were assigned. While time will give us more information on whether the thin-management approach is likely to work consistently, what Philadelphia has shown us is that it *can* work. We attribute that to the fact that the district administration has acted as our partner. It supported our work and didn't try to undermine it. If that kind of cooperation can be replicated, the thin-management model could have legs elsewhere.

The Stockholm Syndrome—on Steroids

When I launched Edison, few understood my real intent. The press, ever quick to land on a simple explanation, largely made this into a private-sector-versus-public-sector story. I can't tell you how many times I've been asked, "So why can the private sector do this better than the public?" Others thought it was some kind of extension of Channel One, expecting that our schools were going to be funded by advertising. I was largely unsuccessful in communicating the most important element in our mission: to bring about a radically new school design, schools that would be fundamentally different from those to which we as a nation were accustomed. Interestingly, we were not only unsuccessful in communicating this but also largely unsuccessful in achieving it. To be very clear, that does not mean we did not bring about *better* schools. (There is a reason school districts bring Edison into their classrooms.) As noted earlier, RAND has confirmed that, in aggregate, those schools partnering with Edison Schools are raising achievement over time at a statistically significant greater rate. That's meaningful. It means tens of thousands of children will graduate who otherwise would not; tens of thousands will go on to better lives than they otherwise could have enjoyed. But as good as Edison's schools are, they are not, in design, nearly as radical in their difference as I had hoped and envisioned.

To the untrained eye, Edison's school design is similar in many ways to the design of all other public schools. The fact that our students still learn largely in classroom settings is one example. Where Edison's schools differ most is in execution, a hard thing to "see" except in results. I've often said that Edison's schools are the "best of the old world" in schools. We've successfully brought together under one school roof many of the best design elements out there. We've been good integrators, and we have relentlessly executed our design. But we have yet to bring about our most important innovation: a school design that provides a highly unusual student and teacher experience and *radically* superior results. We've been largely incremental and quantitative in our departures. And perhaps necessarily so. Many of the great Impressionists were first great masters of convention. Their skill in conventional techniques gave them the credential of "artist," allowing them to depart from accepted ways.

We *have* been revolutionary in two important ways: First, we've built the first national system of public schools managed, collaboratively, by public entities and a private company. Second, those schools have performed better than any other large system of public schools. This is what occupied most of our first decade and a half. And it will act as the launch platform for our next couple of decades. We now have the credentials, the infrastructure, the systems, and the financial strength to do what we originally set out to do: to create radically better schools off radically new designs.

Our inability thus far to innovate in school design on the level that I had hoped has had multiple causes, but one, I believe, is primary: let's call it education's Stockholm syndrome. An incident in Stockholm, Sweden, gave rise to the name. In 1973, following six days of captivity in a bank, a number of hostages became so sympathetic to their captors that they resisted rescue attempts. They even refused to testify against their captors. (Their behavior, analysts believe, was brought about, understandably, by fear. While the motivation of fear does not apply here, the results of their situation do.) The phenomenon of sympathizing with your "captors" exists in public education with the gravitational pull of a collapsing supernova. All of us are "captives" of our own childhood experience—and one of those experiences was "school as we know it," which was imprinted on us with near Intel-like precision. During our most formative years, we "did school" virtually every day. It was such a comprehensive and consuming experience that we find it nearly impossible to imagine that it could be any other way. It is extremely difficult to achieve any separation from the reality that we once knew so incredibly well. Every person setting out to improve schools is a captive of this, including our initial designers.

And even if we could imagine another reality, the existing educational gestalt is seemingly impenetrable. It has an uncanny ability to consume, distort, morph, or deflect any effort to change it. In the movie *Dances with Wolves,* Kevin Costner's character is sent, alone, into the American West in the late 1880s to a remote army outpost and winds up living with a welcoming Indian tribe. So it is with virtually all reform efforts in the world of education. Charter legislation is turned into something it was never intended to be; philanthropic dollars are hijacked in ways the funders could never have imagined; firms such as Edison compromise on design elements that were initially viewed as nonnegotiable. Education is not malevolent, but it is powerfully ingrained.

Yet I am optimistic that the seemingly unchangeable is about to change and that the effort to launch education upward is about to achieve "escape velocity."

I believe we are, as a nation, at a unique moment in the history of schools, a moment that we should not shy away from, indeed, *cannot* shy away from if we are to make our schools what they should and can be. In 1990 America had no serious, large-scale alternative providers of superior public schools. Today we do. The question, then, is how we advance that idea from its beachhead status to something that contributes enormously, comprehensively, and systematically to solving the educational tragedy we see in so many of our schools.

We have learned that it can be done.

The remainder of this book will show how—for Edison Schools and anyone else who cares to venture forth. To business and education readers alike, the fact that I would share strategic insights gleaned from $675 million of investment might appear to be giving away our franchise, in Linux-like form. I am not worried about that for two reasons. First, although ideas make categories, I know that execution, execution, execution is the great differentiator among companies and schools. Second, I care most about a general mobilization toward the ideas that Edison represents. If America and the world come to understand those, then Edison and all its competitors will do just fine—and America's children will do much better.

PART III

Imagining a Better Future for Public Education

INTRODUCTION:
CHANGING THE EDUCATION
PARADIGM

Someone once said that only two institutions in our society remain largely unchanged from the Middle Ages: our schools and our churches. There's significant truth in that statement. Think about it. The basic building block of schools—children in rectangular rooms with a supervising adult in front, teaching from books—has endured for centuries. And as a society we do not believe that it can be very different. Yes, we now know that an oven can be replaced by a microwave, a completely different mechanism of heat. Yes, we learned long ago that rather than driving over or around a great mountain you can tunnel through it (once thought inconceivable). Yes, we've seen that rather than having people walk up stairs, the stairs themselves can move. Yes, we've seen that by cracking something invisibly small (an atom), we can heat (or destroy) an entire city. But schools, well, schools are schools are schools—and forever shall be. Even if failing by the thousands, they are immutable, constant, rigid.

That is about to change, and in a big way.

Unsatisfactory results, technological advances, governmental pressure, earlier puberty, and the introduction of private-sector schooling companies, all these factors are intuitively and constructively coalescing to enable this change. Our old design—and it is largely *one* design used by virtually all U.S. schools—simply doesn't produce the desired result anymore, as Chapter 1 clearly shows. States and the federal government are demanding more for their investments. Puberty, with the rebellion that it brings, comes much earlier now. More and more children are saying to us—often in unsophisticated ways such as acting out or, worse, dropping out—that they want change. (Bill Gates and Michael Dell quit college. Are they trying to tell us something?) Technology— particularly the great advancements in storage, broadband, portability, and costs—now makes possible things we could only dream about a decade ago. Then there are emerging education companies, like Edison, that are able to think in terms of site designs, accountability, systems integration, and scalability. These entities are an important new ingredient in the mix. In the years ahead, they will lead most of the revolutionary design work—not because they are "better" than school-district-based designers but rather and simply because of the inexorable advantages of scale. All these factors are part of a rich brew that is about to result in schools that are not incremental steps from the old ones but rather profound departures, bringing fundamentally different experiences and dramatically improved results to students and teachers alike.

The idea of fundamental new school design made its modern debut in the early 1990s, when both the public and private sectors launched initiatives. Edison Schools conducted the first serious private-sector research-and-development effort on a new school model. Parallel to our effort was the New American Schools initiative—a public/private partnership formed in 1991 through the encouragement of then President Bush and the U.S. Department of Education, under the leadership of Secretary Lamar Alexander. NAS effectively served as a "venture fund" for new school design activity. These were positive events, spawning the largest private-sector involvement in U.S. schooling history and bringing multiple new whole-school designs into the market. But compared with what lies ahead and, more important, compared with what we need, these were fledgling efforts. They were backyard rocket development, not NASA and Redstone Arsenal. They were far from revolutionary in their departures from tradition— and limited in the number of schools that adopted them. But they were and are foundations for future innovation. The two to three decades ahead, when the next generation of designs is conceived and brought to market, will be the most exciting in education history, both qualitatively and quantitatively.

The new designs I speak of could be up and running within a decade, even, in large part, within five years. Nothing stands in their way, not costs, not technology, not unions, not law. Most will be brought to the world in the form of public/private partnerships. Companies, utilizing the advantages of scale, and in a more limited way, nonprofits, will bring these designs about, and school districts will contract with them to either license the design or have the organizations actually manage schools utilizing their designs. When school districts are forced to adhere to old designs because of outdated and unnecessarily restrictive labor agreements or dysfunctional politics, charter schools will spring up in increasing numbers, bringing these new types of schools to achievement-hungry education consumers.

What will these new designs look like? How will they be so different? And what will they cost?

Since money is so critical to every education-reform conversation, let's say a word first about costs. One of the design requirements of schools in the future should be that the cost per pupil does not increase by more than 10 percent in real-dollar terms. Indeed, designers should have a "plan B," which says that the cost of new models must be *equal* to current spending, as that may be the spending reality of the future. Why? As much as we might wish that schools were better funded, we must accept that, in the push and shove around the edges of government coffers, only so much progress can be made. And school-reform advocates must recognize and acknowledge that great increases in public education spending have already been made, in large part because of the tireless and well-organized efforts of unions at the state level. School-district spending has increased at an annual rate of 7 percent in the last twenty-five years, more than double the rate of inflation—with most of the increase going to finance a concurrent and deserved increase in teacher compensation. While the lack of accompanying gains in student achievement might leave us unfulfilled, those historic spending increases actually make additional design- and achievement-based investments harder to achieve. We should keep up the pressure on states to devote more dollars to new designs, because, well spent, dollars do and will matter. But to expect dramatic rises, (1) after two decades of unparalleled growth in education budgets, (2) after less than satisfactory returns on those investments (to say the least), and (3) when the country is about to confront the costs related to its aging population, well, that expectation is not realistic. Even a 10 percent increase in real spending is daunting. The design changes I am about to advocate could be realized for a 10 percent increase in U.S. education spending—with the great bulk of that money appropriated *after* the new designs are developed and up and running in the marketplace. (And in a push, these changes could be done for current dollars.) The best way to find increases in funding, particularly in the future, is to show lawmakers a whole new level of promise (and then results) coming from new designs.

This will require a new way of thinking. New designs need not be spend-at-all-costs pipe dreams. Education is one of the few sectors of American life where people reflexively believe that quality and effectiveness can *only* be achieved with more money. Implicit in the public statements of many education policy makers is a presumption that the measure of commitment to improved education is the amount of money spent. In some sectors and industries, the genetic "wiring" is exactly the reverse—that is, institutions know that only through increasing quality and effectiveness at *lower* costs will they be able to stay in business. Think virtually the entire technology industry. The automotive industry. Wal-Mart. Consider what has happened to the cost of computers. Today you can buy a computer with enhanced power and performance for a fraction of the cost of five years ago. The knee-jerk reaction is that this kind of thinking doesn't apply to education— that education is a labor-intensive industry where costs simply cannot be decreased without negatively impacting quality. New school designers will not—and should not—accept that premise.

So, knowing that by both necessity and desire we should keep the costs of new designs at or within spitting distance of our current costs, what will these new schools look like?

There will be many variations, but schools of our near future will contain certain themes—essential elements necessary to advance our schools to a new level. In this part of the book, Chapter 5 introduces ideas that show a very different type of engagement of students in their own education and in their schools. Chapter 6 focuses on how the staffs of future schools will be very different. Chapter 7 is a collection of additional ideas that could well be important in future school designs. And Chapter 8 provides three scenarios of the potential implementation of such new designs in the coming years.

I do not claim ownership of any of these ideas. Some already exist in various schools. Some might be under development here and there. Educators could be hard at work on particular elements to be discussed. But I know that the *average* U.S. school at best has only one or two of these in effect—probably without great support or design. I have neither seen nor heard of a school in America with all these elements in place.

I'm not arguing that all schools in the United States should incorporate these new elements. I'm not saying that the country needs "one school design." I'm not saying that I have identified a complete list of new ingredients for future schools—or even the right ones. What I'm saying is this: This country will not get the kind of educational results it wants and needs unless it radically changes the way it goes about schooling, unless virtually all schools incorporate major new elements. My goal is to stimulate your imagination—and your involvement in rethinking how our schools should be designed.

CHAPTER 5

Student Uprising

Independent Learning—A Class Action Suit Against "Classes Only"

The element of school design is, perhaps, the most crucial. It is the feature that most distinguishes schools of the future from schools of today—and that will enable other parts of the design. In particular, without the implementation of this element, the large-scale increases in teacher and principal pay, to be suggested later, cannot happen.

As was mentioned briefly earlier, today's default "national school design" is so ingrained in our national psyche that most people are not even aware of the group of almost religious assumptions upon which it is based. All of us went through the current design, most for twelve years (think twelve years of imprinting), making it difficult to imagine that a school experience could be particularly different. Here are some of the things that most of us treat as "fixed" realities:

1. **In school, children must be supervised by adults virtually all of the time.** Ask yourself: During your schooling experience, what percentage of time did you spend outside the supervision of an adult? If it was over 5 percent, you went to a very unusual school. The assumption here, speaking bluntly, is that children must be forced to learn, that left to their own devices they would never do it, that they would flee from schools cheering, just as they do at the end of most school days. Is their fleeing a result of some anti-education gene—or could it be, even just a little bit, that they are running from something they experience as ineffective and wasteful? Could it be that they are fleeing from something they view as educational assault and battery? Could it also be that under different circumstances, they would gladly stay?

2. **The school day must be rather rigidly organized, generally chopped up into 45-minute or one-hour blocks.** The idea that these blocks might be two hours was, some years ago, viewed as a grand breakthrough. Ask yourself: During your schooling experience, did you ever have large blocks of time that you organized yourself?

3. **The smaller the number of children in a class, the better the educational results.** Virtually all U.S. adults believe this. But ask yourself why you believe this. Which would be better, a bad teacher with fifteen kids or a good one with thirty? You might have heard that Japan has educational results superior to ours. Did you know that class sizes in Japan are much larger than those of the United States?

4. **Adults must run all aspects of the school—and do the work within it.** Students are there to be "served." Schools carry students; students don't carry schools.

———

What if all of the above "truths" are incorrect—truths that we will someday regard as myths, artifacts of a forgotten era? What if we approached the organization of a school *without* any of these "truths" as cornerstones? Where might simple logic and our own experiences take us instead? What would a school look like then? More important, how would that school perform, not just in the narrow sense of standardized test scores (though in those for sure), but also in the broader sense of developing well-rounded, highly skilled young adults?

Let me give you some of what the new truths of school design might be. Let's focus on five:

1. Learning accomplished through individual effort, or through working in small teams, is "stickier" (better retained) than that "served up" in any group, no matter what size.
2. Learning can come in many forms, and the size of the learning group can vary greatly without any penalization of effect whatsoever.
3. Children are capable of tremendous focus and responsibility on their own, and they can be taught these traits earlier than you might think.
4. Variety also matters in learning. Too much of any one thing, like sitting reactively in a classroom for twelve years, has rapidly diminishing returns. (And teachers need variety, too.)
5. Children can teach as well as learn. Has your child ever taught you anything? Has your older child ever taught one of your younger ones?

So working from these new potential "truths," let's imagine what a school of the future might look like. Let's suppose, for example, that beginning *in the first grade* children were expected to spend an hour a day learning on their own, not under the direct supervision of a teacher (though perhaps watched over by one of their older peers). Or let's assume they were *not in class* for one hour a day. Let's presume that by the third grade, the amount of time in which students were "on their own" had increased to two hours per day. By the sixth grade and throughout middle school, let's assume, only *half* of a student's time was spent in what we now think of as a classroom. Finally, by high school, imagine that only *one-third* of a student's time was in a traditional classroom setting. (If you think this is overly radical, consider that many college students are in class fewer than fifteen hours a week. They are only a few months older than high school seniors. Did something magically occur to make them more capable of independent learning?)

What, you may be asking, are these students doing? Sleeping at their desks? Playing video games on the school's computers? And if they are not with teachers, then where are they? Have they fled the school entirely?

Well, the answer is: *They are learning,* just not, at that very moment, with a teacher, just not in a class. More often than not, they will be reading! (Educators believe deeply that students should be reading, but how much of the school day do we actually allow them to do that? We say they should read in the evening, but realistically, after a long day at school and with other homework and important activities, do we really believe they can or will?) They also will be working with a small group of other students. And they might be on their computers, *writing,* researching, exploring, mining that almost endless, great new ethereal library, the Internet.

As for *where* they are: they are in their own cubbies, just as they will probably be years later in their entry-level jobs. (This, by the way, doesn't mean that old schools have to be completely rehabbed. Just imagine that some existing classrooms are converted into rooms filled with thirty "learning spots." New schools,

though, would have a completely new architectural design to ac-
commodate the emergence of large-scale independent learning.)

Many educators reading this are probably saying, perhaps in less
kindly terms, "This idea is hopelessly naïve. Students cannot be
entrusted with their own educations; they cannot be expected to
manage their own time. Students don't understand the importance
of education and, therefore, can't be expected to manage it."

My response: Schools have failed to make students the masters
of their own learning, and we have the results to show for it. We
are still operating in a type of Charles Dickens mindset, believing
that these young, half-civilized things called children must be literally whipped into shape, if not by a stick then by a never-ending
schedule. If students don't understand the importance of education enough to take charge of their own, it is because the schools
we have designed don't spend any real time helping them understand this. Worse, because it has been so long since we examined
the real rationale of our schools, perhaps schools themselves
don't even understand why we are teaching as we do. One of the
first things schools should teach is *why education is important.* If we
do that well, students will embrace their own education. They will
become the school's most important teachers: their own.

So how do we operationalize this new independent model? What
are some of the mechanisms that bring it about? Here are some
key ingredients:

First, students must be taught how to work on their own, beginning in the early grades. This skill must be part of their education, and a part of the curriculum. And this "independence"
should be celebrated by teachers early on—so that it becomes
something younger students eagerly anticipate.

Second, though students should be doing a great deal of learning on their own, the independent work should be completely linked to their time in class with teachers. Class should be illumination and discussion that inspires further inquiry. Independent time should be spent reading, researching, exploring, and gaining depth on the classroom topics, as well as getting stumped and needing the teacher's help. There should be a seamlessness between class and independent learning.

Third, new curricula will be required—though, in a push, the old can be modified. One interesting way to think about new texts in this design is to give students both the text *and* the teacher's guide. If, to a degree, students are going to teach themselves, then why not give them a teacher's resources? Another interesting possibility is that schools adopt or adapt the curriculum now being used by homeschooling organizations, the ultimate "independent learning" entities, if you will. Schools of the future could, in effect, become a hybrid, operating in part under our current "brick and mortar" design and in part like new "virtual schools." Early experiments in this hybrid are already under way.

Fourth, a ubiquitous, superbly functioning technological backbone will be required—that is, laptops for all, and robust networks. Much of the independent work will be through the Internet. And one way teachers will monitor progress is through technology—students will be filing electronic reports, doing electronic assessments, and so on.

The fifth element is an important "bridge" for those who cannot leave behind the mooring that students must be supervised. Specifically, student "prefects" or parent "monitors" would be an important part of the new independent learning community. Think of them being "on patrol," no different from monitors at crosswalks, to ensure that students have ready access to help and keep moving forward constructively.

Of all the things that this book proposes, independent learning could have the greatest single "educational effect." The reason: What can be more important than schools graduating students who are capable of independent work? Being literate is one thing. It is quite another to be self-motivated, self-organized, self-disciplined, self-confident. Though these traits can develop in the current, centuries-old, always-in-a-classroom design that we now deploy, logic and our own life experiences tell us these characteristics will mature more quickly in an environment specifically designed to nurture them—an environment where independence is taught, expected, and practiced. It might not be something that is directly measured on a state assessment, but any reader of this book knows how important it is to success in life.

Student Motivation—Systems of Hope

Several years ago, when Edison decided to take its stock public, I had to learn all about becoming a public company. (I had, for nearly thirty years, run private companies and had no real experience in the public markets.) I immediately launched into my own course of study, mainly asking endless questions of investment bankers and investors and reading everything I could find on the topic. You might say that I was a very motivated learner. Why? I knew that in order to accomplish certain objectives, I had to master this material. There was nothing "theoretical" about it. An IPO was on the horizon, and to conduct it successfully, I had to be educated in this arena. From a teacher's standpoint, I was the best of students. I knew *why* I needed to learn. And thus I was completely motivated, eager to learn, and prepared to work to do it.

How many of America's students are in a similar mindset? Some are, to be sure. They have a certain love for learning, sparked perhaps by their parents or an inspiring teacher. But most students—in my experience, the great majority—are in school because they have to be. Many, probably most, are attending for negative reasons rather than positive ones: because there will be disapproval from teachers and parents if they do not; because they will not get into a good college; or because they will suffer the embarrassment of an F. Most have only an inkling of the positive opportunity education can bring them, or how crucial schooling is to their happiness. They do not have that full appreciation because schools have failed to provide it to them. Motivation is not part of our standard curriculum. Very simply, our schools do an absolutely miserable job of showing students *why* education is important. Premise: If we were to do that and do it really well, we would see a mammoth leap in the country's educational performance. If schools are a ship and only teachers row, you go at one speed. If everyone is rowing, what a difference! You get wherever you are going much faster (and cheaper, too).

The problem here is palpable and easy to see—hard to miss, in fact. Visit a school that serves students from kindergarten through twelfth grade. It is a study in contrasts. Visit the younger grades first. At that level, schools don't have to worry about the motivation issue. School is new, an adventure for children. As educators, we're still surfing on the natural desire of these kids to explore, to find out. But then go directly to a middle school or high school class and you can literally *see* a drop in the level of energy and engagement. The children are leaning back, not forward. There is a tactile listlessness to classes. You can feel it. Participation is limited, awkward. It is easy to say this is just adolescence, yet adolescence is not always so—a fact made very clear by a trip to the lunchroom in the same school. There, energy abounds.

So what does a school do about the motivation of its students? Answer: We must make the motivation of students a part of our school design and our national curriculum. We should teach it; help students find it; assess it; track it. But how? Six things, to start.

First, every school year should begin with ceremonies that are about the *why* of school. Just as a coach gathers players in the locker room for one final pep talk before each and every game, just as a company commander rallies troops on the crucial nature of a battle, and just as a company CEO often addresses the organization's staff at pivotal points in a company's progress, so should the principal and staff of a school gather students at the outset of a year to illuminate the importance of the work they will be doing. The program should not be written or planned the night before but rather viewed as the most important address a principal and staff will make to students. Themes should be introduced (slogans don't hurt, either) that will be reiterated from time to time during the year.

Second, schools should also look to spark and jump-start the motivation of students with a subtler, less direct method: methodically exposing children to greatness, excellence, success in many fields and then emphasizing how learning was important to each example. Every day every school should put excellence on display (and school systems should aid them in doing this).

Third, *every* course should begin with a thoughtful discussion led by the teacher on *why* that particular course is important to students and *why* excelling in the course is better than meandering through it. This should not be done in five minutes. It should be, at least, the entire opening session and perhaps the first two or three sessions of a course. (And, as booster shots, a teacher should remind students of its relevance along the way during the course.) Good curriculum providers should build this into what they provide, making it easier for teachers to accomplish.

Fourth, every day should touch on the *why.* Just a sentence or a paragraph on how the lesson of the day matters. "Why" should become a standard, built-in part of good teaching.

Fifth, as much as we should find and stoke motivation, it is equally important that we not kill it. When something we are teaching is just mindless, we should stop doing it. Or if we must teach children something so that they can pass some equally mindless exam, then it's best that we admit it. Better that students know we know. I'll give you an example. I run a reasonably complex $400+ million company, and I cannot recall needing most of the higher-math material that I learned. I know that statement is heresy, but ask yourself: If 99 percent of children are not going to use it, why is it, again, that we're teaching it? (If the answer is that it helps them to learn in a more general sense or identifies those with particular aptitudes, let's let them know that.)

Finally, as the saying goes, you do what you measure, so we should measure the motivation of students. A good school of the future should annually assess the motivation of its children. It would be simple enough. An annual, well-developed survey of children could ask questions like:

1. Do you find school interesting?
2. Do you enjoy school?
3. How would you rate the importance and relevance of each class you took this year?
4. Do you think school will make a difference in your success?
5. Did your teachers do a good job of helping you see why school is important?

If the absolute scores on these questions are low or not moving up, it will tell a school and its leadership something they don't now know. And as you read these questions, is it not clear that they are important?

One final thing about student motivation: School is getting us ready for life—and a very important part of life is our work. Now ask yourself: Do schools devote any significant time to showing our students what the real world of work is, what the hundreds of options are? Schools of the future will begin to introduce students, early on, to that world in a "spiraling" survey course that begins in elementary school and continues throughout their educational career. If students cannot see where all their effort leads, how can we expect them to work hard? "General pep talks" will not lead to highly motivated learners. Students must make tangible connections to their future, so they can see and feel what they might be working toward. And parents can be a great help in this matter. They are out in that real world every day. So why not import them back to school, as a key part of communicating to our children what work is all about?

Students Run the School

One day years ago, my then five-year-old son had a splinter in his finger. For ten minutes, I tried to get it out with tweezers, amid his squirming and crying. Finally, in frustration I said, "Well, just do it yourself!" He took the tweezers without hesitation, and within five seconds and without a word of complaint, the splinter was out. The lesson: Kids can do more than we think—if we just let them. More important, they learn from doing. Indeed, I believe actual work, the doing of something, is one of the best ways to learn. From the trying, the failing, the finally getting it right, we imprint lessons onto our mental hard drives in a way that "classroom learning" cannot equal. As I look back on my youth, I appreciate how much I learned from my jobs, in and out of schools. I was not much of a student, but I was a terrific worker, before, during, and after school, and from this work I learned much of what I know and use today. Three paper routes taught me discipline (getting up every day at 5 A.M. from age eight to twelve has a way of sticking with you). Pumping gas taught me that I did not want to do that and made me appreciate more those who do. Being a waiter brought me organization skills (such as how to sequence five tables that arrive simultaneously). And waiting tables has made me a nicer patron for life, having seen firsthand plenty of bad ones. Campaigning for student body president in high school and college taught me more about public speaking than any course ever did.

If, then, work is a great teacher, ask yourself this: Are we employing work as an educational strategy in our schools to great effect? Further, is it possible that permitting students to play central roles in the actual operation of our schools could enhance not only their own education but that of other children as well?

Today, most schools assign a few tasks to students. Some teachers will appoint students to collect papers. Some principals will assign students to serve as administrative aides or messengers in the school office. Athletics is actually pretty advanced on this front, with coaches recruiting student managers, statisticians, and so on. But I have never seen or heard of a *comprehensive*, robust program to involve students in the actual "work of a school," and I am convinced that this idea has great educational promise. In particular, I think it can enhance the education of the individual student, increase the overall performance of the school, and finally, save school funds, which could then be invested to greater educational effect.

Let's imagine that every school of the future had a program

called Student Chores. For purposes of this discussion, let's consider what that program might look like in a 900-student, K–8
school.

Imagine that this school has developed and described a list of
50 different chores. Each student selects and performs 27 of
these (each for three months) over the nine years at the school, as
both a part of his or her education and a contribution to the
school. (If parents object to this program, their child can opt
out.) A student has a chore for one hour, three days a week. For
each chore, there is a brief training program to orient the student
to his or her assigned role. (If, at this point, you are wondering
who will manage all this, the entire Student Chores program will
probably be managed *by the students themselves*—that is, running the
Chores program would be a chore in and of itself, with one of the
upper-grade duties being the training and coaching of younger
students in their chores.)

Each chore has an educational objective—a standard that
students are expected to master. Some of these standards tie in
with educational standards of the state, while others relate more
to preparing students for work later in life. Each chore is periodically monitored and assessed, preferably even graded. In states
with relatively high funding levels for education, students are even
paid a small amount for their chores. The type of chore increases
in complexity as students increase in age.

So exactly what will students be doing in the school? The most
important chore is tutoring, with fifth-graders helping first-graders,
eighth-graders helping fifth-graders, and so forth. Students are
assigned tutoring tasks based on their own strengths. Example:
Students earning A and B grades in math make up the bulk of the
school's math tutors, those receiving A and B grades in reading
are reading tutors, and so forth. Language tutors are drawn significantly from native language speakers. Children whose first lan-

guage is Spanish are effectively the assistant teachers of Spanish, and students whose first language is English reciprocate in a similar fashion. The road to a multicultural nation will be accelerated by the children of each culture teaching one another.

To give you an example of how educationally powerful this single chore of tutoring could be, imagine that the top 20 percent of students in the school, and only from the fourth grade up, are assigned a chore of one hour of tutoring, three days per week. Five hundred students × 20 percent = 100 students × 3 hours per week = 300 hours per week. Three hundred hours of tutoring per week is the equivalent of adding 7.5 *full-time tutors* to a school. A typical K–8 school with 900 students has a teaching force of about 60. Adding the equivalent of 7.5 members to the team is nearly a 12.5 percent increase in instructional manpower, and so far we've deployed only a small portion of the student power in a school.

Before outlining what other chores might be, let's take a moment to quantify what one hour per student three times a week actually means to the manpower of a school. The bottom line is this: *It's the equivalent of doubling the full-time teaching positions.* Here's the calculation: Assuming a 900-student K–8 school and assuming one hour of chores per student three days a week, you wind up with a total weekly count of 2,700 hours. At 40 hours per week, that is the equivalent of adding *67 full-time staff positions to a school.* A typical K–8 school with 900 students has about that number of teaching positions. Obviously, a full-time equivalent composed of a cadre of students is not the same as a professional adult, but the impact on the school and its workload would be considerable. And a Student Chores program could have a positive effect on the school's budget, perhaps freeing up funds for increased teacher pay or a new technology infrastructure.

What, in addition to tutoring, might students do? The truth is, there is very little they can*not* do in a school by a certain age. Let's examine just a few possible chores in more detail.

At home when your computer has a glitch, whom do you turn to for help, your twelve-year-old or your spouse? Answer: the twelve-year-old. Why? Because twelve-year-olds know more about a computer than most adults will ever learn. Why, then, can students not become the arms and legs of the tech staff in a school? (Most schools, by the way, are lucky to have one full-time tech person, a person who is often overwhelmed by the job of keeping the school computers and networks functioning.) This student tech force could do small computer repairs, install and remove software, develop and maintain the school "home page," update databases, serve as the "help desk" for students who are having problems (even for an hour in the evening from home), and "tutor" younger students on the proper use of computers. And remember, these students would be learning *constantly*, increasing their own computer skills through this chore.

Let's go to the school office. Students could answer phones, run in-school errands, confirm appointments (such as parent-teacher conferences) with parents, conduct school tours, and manage print jobs. (This is already done in many schools.)

Other chores could include aiding teachers in various administrative functions (yes, even grading); aiding in parent programs (including recruiting parents to volunteer at the school); serving as hallway monitors for study halls, lunchrooms, and hallways; assisting in various safety functions (bus loading aides/crossing guards); and keeping the school yard free of litter (a favorite in such programs in Japan and an incentive not to litter yourself).

Finally, remember from the above section all those students who are engaged in independent learning? Who is monitoring them? If an eighth-grader can babysit children *alone* at home, why can't he or she monitor (with a walkie-talkie in case of need) younger students engaged in independent learning? And is that not great preparation for future supervisory roles?

Aside from the learning and economic benefits, there are two other major advantages to a robust chores program. First, it greatly enhances the culture of a school, with students developing a keen sense of "ownership." Second, one of the great side benefits of a chores program is the teaching of responsibility to our children. Every chore would be structured to teach the dignity of work—that there is honor in a job well done, whatever it might be.

A concluding note on this idea might also convey how difficult ideas such as this are to introduce. At an Edison company meeting some years ago, I was speaking on ideas for future school design and included an earlier version of this concept. It was a large meeting for company clients and staff only, but a reporter well known to be an opponent of the company was lurking outside the conference hall trying to hear through the doorway. The next day his article announced that Edison was introducing child labor. The article attempted to convince readers that Edison intended to use abusive child labor practices in order to cut costs and reduce adult jobs. This characterization, then and now, is simply ridiculous, as the above description of this concept should make clear. It is, however, an instructive example of how new and potentially good ideas can be distorted by poor, slanted reporting and/or vested interests.

CHAPTER 6

Next-Level Educators

Next-Level Leaders

There are more than 90,000 public schools in America. On average, the principal of each of those schools holds in his or her hands the formative years of roughly 500 of our children, more than the number of "souls on board" a typical 747. Anyone who has been around schooling very long knows this: An underperforming principal guarantees an underperforming school, and a good one gives you a chance at a good school. Principals are one of the key leverage points within a school. That leads the school designer to many questions. Who do we want our principals to be? What do we want them to know? Where do we expect them to come from? How do we want them developed? How should we attract them? What should we pay them? Once again, let's start with the money: how we must change principal pay in America.

Look at this chart:

PAY COMPARABLES	
POSITION	TYPICAL ANNUAL PAY RANGE
Physician (IM)	$175,000–$250,000
747 captain	$240,000–$275,000
Hospital head	$135,000–$200,000
Large-store manager	$120,000–$200,000
Principal	$75,000–$85,000

If the above pay structure holds, only those prepared to make a dramatic economic sacrifice will be our schools' leaders. Thousands of those heroic individuals are out there—they make up the best of our principal corps today—but are there 90,000 of them? History and our record of school performance tell us no. So either we dramatically increase the pay of our school leaders *or* we accept the inevitable result.

What's interesting is that we *can,* as a society, increase principals' pay rather easily. Let's assume there are 90,000 principals with an average pay of $80,000 each. That means we spend about $7.2 billion per year in principal compensation, or just 1.75 percent of total annual expenditure on K–12 education. The math is pretty simple: we could increase principal pay in the United States to $200,000 per year by adding to or reallocating just over 2.6 percent of annual K–12 spending. We could finance this investment by directing a portion of our annual education spending increases to it. Or we could find the money through reallocation of our existing educational dollars, something I'll show later.

But let's talk about it, for a moment, in terms of the return on investment we would get. Five years ago, Edison Schools had the idea of a pleasant surprise for its absolutely best-performing principals. We decided to award them with red Mustang convertibles, cars costing about $25,000. We determined that a principal had to make a gain rate in student achievement of over 10 percent (at that time, 3 to 5 times national norms) and also meet his or her school budget in order to win one of the cars. In other words, they had to both deliver for children and be frugal with taxpayer money.

We were worried that this idea might get negative press. "For-Profit Company Gives Away Flashy Cars to Principals" was the kind of headline we could imagine. But we were convinced that serious incentives could drive school performance, so we just sucked it up and did it anyway. We could not have imagined the reaction when we announced the principals who had achieved this, inviting them to the stage. They and all their colleagues were stunned that they were being recognized at this level. They could not believe we were actually doing it. They thought it was a prank. We immediately decided to institutionalize this idea, and rather than cars we now award principals achieving this status an annual check, above and beyond bonuses for other levels of performance. Guess what has happened? Each year the number of principals coming to the stage at our annual awards dinner has grown. Now top Edison principals receive bonuses in the $25,000 to $35,000 class. (In thousands of U.S. school districts, there is no incentive award for principals at all, and where there is, it tends to be marginal—for example, 3 percent of base.) Some districts are experimenting—using, for example, philanthropic funds to pay bonuses. But for all practical purposes, *serious* principal performance compensation does not exist.

And guess what has happened to Edison's student performance over that same period. When we began this program, our annual gain rate was about 4 percent, at that time roughly double national averages. In the 2003–2004 school year, the gain rate nearly doubled, to 8 percent! Many things contributed to that increase, but we view principal compensation awards as one of the key factors. If our principal compensation system were only one-fourth of the reason our performance doubled—and I suspect it is more—that would mean that an increase of 2 percent in spending drove 25 percent of our increase in performance. That's a good return on investment—and that's by increasing principal pay by only 30 percent. What would happen if we more than doubled principal pay in America? What if America paid its great principals $200,000 per year?

I'm not recommending that we increase principal compensation to an average base salary of $200,000 per year. My recommendation would be that, as a nation, we increase average base pay for principals to about $120,000 with bonus potential of up to $80,000 per year, paid out strictly based on achievement performance measures. (At Edison, we have a quantitative system that measures five factors and pays bonuses accordingly. In descending order of importance, the factors measured are: student achievement, financial management, school design, "customer satisfaction" [parents, teachers, students], and operational excellence.)

Two other benefits would accrue from this approach:

First, the overall candidate pool of principals would increase dramatically. Someone in the future would have to consider that a principal could receive as much financial reward as many lawyers, as all but the highest-paid pilots, or as very well-paid middle managers in thousands of private-sector companies. Over time, the pool of candidates from which we could choose would exponentially increase. And that would affect the quality of leadership.

Second, principal turnover in the United States plagues our schools generally. The problem is worse at the toughest schools, where achievement is most lacking. It is not unusual for a challenging school to have a new principal every one or two years. Worse, such a school may not even have a principal—it may have only an interim leader because a qualified one cannot be found. Principal turnover is even higher than teacher turnover. Given the demands of these posts, many principals simply conclude that it's not worth it and trade in their skills for greater rewards elsewhere. (And the best of them know that their management skills are worth a lot more in other sectors.) Given that it takes years to build a great school culture, this pattern has debilitating effects. As principal pay increases, turnover will decline.

One other note: We should execute the same proportional level of increased compensation for the nation's superintendents. Leaders of our school systems should receive performance bonuses equivalent to 100 percent of their base pay *if* they are significantly moving student achievement ahead. But that's a system-level design issue, not a school-level one.

If significant increases in principal pay will meaningfully increase the quality of candidate pools, then better principal education and training will get candidates ready to lead great schools.

I hear again and again from principals that the course work they did to become a principal was primarily theoretical and often not "on point." They say their training did little to prepare them for the actual role of running a 600- to 1,000-student institution with 50 to 100 staff members and a budget of $4 million to $10 million per year. At the end of the day, most say, they just picked up their training on the job.

How can we expect great schools if our school managers are not purposefully trained to produce them? Shouldn't we have "principal colleges" that look more like medical schools, that are as rigorous as law schools, and that are as practical as flight schools—and just as selective? Shouldn't we have in education the equivalent of Annapolis, West Point, and the Air Force Academy to educate the "company commanders" of our world-class schools? And as in the field of medicine, shouldn't the notion of "internship" be more formalized?

I'll say "yes" to all those questions. And go a lot further than that. The federal government should jump-start the launch of five new state-of-the-art principal universities, a point that I'll talk more about later in this book.

In less than a decade, America's educational system can transform the leadership corps of public schools through greater compensation and far more rigorous education of principals. And it can do that for affordable investments within the structure of our current funding system.

A New Level of Professionalism for Teachers

In America's great universities, the title "full professor" is bestowed after considerable scrutiny by those who grant it and much effort by those who seek it. In law, you must pass the bar—and then, if you work very hard for a number of years, you might become partner in a prestigious firm. In medicine, it takes six to eight long and arduous years after college before you practice independently, and that's if you don't specialize. And in all these fields, for all this effort and education, you can be rewarded handsomely. Surgeons can earn north of $500,000 per year; partners in top American law firms can do that and more; and even professors at major universities, when one considers income from research and consulting activities, can approach that number.

Contrast that with America's K–12 teachers. In many cities one can literally walk in off the street and get a job, without one day of formal education in the science and art of teaching. Given that degree of selectivity, is it surprising that pay is *on average* only $46,000? Understandably, because of teacher shortage there is a movement toward "alternative certification" of teachers. An inescapable message is "Teaching is something you can kind of pick up. Anyone can really do it." What does that tell us? How would we feel about "alternative certification" for pilots? Or surgeons?

Teaching is a profession; it's just often not treated like one in America. Though as a society we "talk it up," our actions don't bear out our so-called beliefs. It doesn't have to be like that, and it will not be in schools of the future. We need to pay our teachers much more—and we need to prepare them much better for the complexity of their roles. Let's begin, as we did with principals, with pay.

When I grew up in the 1950s, in prefeminist times, teachers in our schools were virtually all women, many of whom, today, would be lawyers, doctors, and business executives. Those fields were not, for the most part, open to them. The result was that America's schools had an enormous talent pool and an "artificial marketplace" for talent. Because women had few alternative opportunities in those days, schools did not pay them their true worth. One of the unintended consequences of equal rights for women was an exodus of this talent from our schools. Education, in one sense, was a "protected industry"—protected not by taxes on imports but by financial injustice to the women who served it so well for decades. When the higher-end job markets were finally opened to women, and schools did not respond with comparably increased compensation, there was an enormous loss of talent, no different from the way removing governmental protections from an import-sensitive industry would drastically affect its ability to compete.

As with principals, there is enormous capability in many of America's classrooms. Many teachers, who could take their talents elsewhere for much higher pay, choose to make an economic sacrifice to serve children and the country. They are, in effect, philanthropists, and we as a nation are in their debt. But aside from the inherent unfairness of this situation, it is not a scalable model. It is not reasonable to expect 3 million people (the number of teachers in public K–12 schools) to make this sacrifice every year for decades. The result: Many teachers in our classrooms are less qualified than we would like. Or said another way: Except in those cases where people are making an economic sacrifice, we too often get what we pay for.

If we want a certain level of talent in our classrooms, we must pay for it. And unlike pay increases for principals, the adjustment is not going to be a small one in absolute terms. Unions in this country fight for 3 percent and 5 percent annual increases in teacher compensation. That's an important contribution, but we need to understand that a 5 percent increase is not going to get the job done. Let's be clear: *we need to double or triple teacher pay in the United States.* If we believe good teaching is as important to society as good lawyering or good health care (and just about as complicated—which it is), then we're going to have to reward it accordingly, or at least nearly so. So what does that mean? The average U.S. teacher earns $46,000 today. The lowest-paid teachers should be able to earn today's average—straight out of college. The highest-paid should earn $130,000 or more, a number that should be reserved not for those with the grayest hair but those with greatest performance, whatever their hair color. That level of pay will move teaching from a field that requires a quasi vow of poverty (barely middle-class life) to one that attracts not only those who care but also those who have plenty of other options.

Just as in law, medicine, business, and virtually every other profession, compensation must be keyed to performance and responsibility, not seniority. The concept that everyone should be paid the same regardless of results and, basically, on an hourly basis, is the single greatest indication of the backwardness of the field. More than anything else it undermines the label of "profession," reducing it instead to the equivalent of any number of services that rely solely on "time on task," not "true delivery."

In most schools today, teachers are teachers are teachers. In most collective-bargaining agreements, a central premise is little differentiation in either pay or responsibility based on teaching ability. The key differentiators are (1) how long one has taught and (2) how many degrees in education one has. Many new school designs of the past decade, including that of Edison Schools, have begun to challenge this construct, providing different teachers with different levels of responsibility and differentiated pay. But the "old plan" remains a central feature in the great majority of U.S. schools. In part this is so because of the weight of convention. In part it is because union leaders have made uniformity a top collective-bargaining priority, judging that differentiation is too risky for their members—and their own leadership positions.

Schools of the future will take the pioneering efforts of some of the early designs of the 1990s, improve them, and more important, extend them from hundreds of schools to thousands. Look at the following chart as one example of how our teaching forces might be structured:

Having responsibility structures is not a new idea. Edison first proposed something similar to these a decade ago. But we never dared propose anything as "rich" as the pay rates shown in the chart on page 126. Even if funding were available, such a structure would be disallowed under most collective-bargaining agreements. And where it might be allowed, the only way to progress would be through tenure—the longest tenure gets you the lead

A New Teaching Staff Construct*

Title/Experience	Responsibility	Base Pay	Performance Bonus	Total Comp
Teacher intern (directly out of college)	Classroom teaching, with significant coaching by lead and senior teachers	$38,000	$8,000	$46,000
Teacher (2+ years)	Classroom teaching, largely independently	$50,000	$16,500	$66,500
Senior teacher (player/coach) (5+ years)	Classroom teaching *and* coaching within subject specialties	$65,000	$25,000	$90,000
Lead teacher (player/coach/manager) (7–10+ years)	Classroom teaching (though somewhat lighter load) *and* coaching and managing a team of teachers (a house). A middle-management position within the school.	$85,000	$45,000	$130,000

*Actual salaries will vary from location to location.

teacher spot. In new school designs, there will be little, if any, limit on how rapidly one progresses to the rank of lead teacher. In reality, it will take some time, perhaps seven years, before one has the experience and skills, but it will not be unusual to see some twenty-eight-year-old lead teachers and some fifty-five-year-old ones as well. In every sense of the word, it will be a meritocracy.

As shown in the chart, the potential increase in teachers' pay is dramatic. Most of the increase comes from performance-based compensation, however. And as with principal salaries, the higher the total potential teacher compensation, the greater the performance-oriented percentage. To date, the few experiments in performance-based compensation for public school teachers have virtually all been plagued by a lack of funding that constrains the size of a bonus. A $1,000 bonus potential on a $46,000 base will not materially alter behavior. But imagine the power of a $15,000 bonus potential on a $46,000 base. That has the ability to attract a teacher's attention and drive results.

And what should the criteria for performance be? Eighty percent of teacher performance bonuses should be based on the achievement gains of children. Systems for accurate measurement of annual achievement gains by individual children are rapidly being put in place on a state-by-state basis across the United States. These should be the primary objective measurement for performance pay. (And America should not accept that we do not have the methods to administer such a system fairly.) A secondary criterion should be adherence to the particular curriculum protocols of the schools. Teachers should be rewarded for utilizing clear best practices instead of "freelancing" with favorite protocols that have not been shown by research to work. If history is a guide, unions will resist most of the above design changes in teacher compensation. They don't like highly differentiated teacher responsibility (particularly the idea of lead teachers acting as managers over new, less experienced teachers), and even more so, they don't like performance pay. For these reasons, these changes are likely to first come about in charter schools free of collective-bargaining arrangements and in states where collective-bargaining agreements don't exist. I say "first come about" because it is clear to me that once pay that is much higher and much more performance-based is put effectively in place in significant numbers of schools, union resistance to it will quickly crumble. That will happen because the rank and file will revolt, desiring and deserving the higher compensation they will see their colleagues receiving. It will be an East Berlin/West Berlin phenomenon—an unsustainable situation for those on the other side of the wall. Also, over time, union leadership will recognize that this is not a threat to their organizations.

But a question you are already asking is, How does America fund a doubling of average teacher salaries? Increasing principal pay is one thing. But there are 3 million teachers in public schools today, together earning about $138 billion per year. If you double their pay, you might ask, didn't you just spend $138 billion, an increase of approximately 33 percent of the total U.S. K–12 education budget? Answer: no. Reason: Schools of the future will employ far fewer teachers than schools today.

The teacher union leaders reading this book just keeled over, believing that a large portion of their dues just went away and that class size just increased. Wrong on both counts. If the dues of every teacher were to increase pro rata with teacher pay, union revenue would be kept whole and union "profit margins" would actually improve, as they would have fewer members to serve. And class size would stay more or less constant, because there would be fewer classes in schools of the future. (Remember from the previous chapter that in the future students will work independently "out of class" for significant portions of the time.) The "horrors" that unions imagine happen only if you believe that the structure of schools is rigid, that the day must be divided into six classes, that children must always be in a class with an adult, and that classes must always be smaller to be better. In short, one has to believe that schooling, unlike almost every other human endeavor, is a fixed design, impervious to innovation and creativity. But designers of schools of the future will not blindly accept any of those particular dogmas. They will see a new way. To put it differently, there was a time in aviation when the propeller was the only way to move a plane forward. Designers could not envision getting beyond a certain speed with a prop. Then came jet engines, and the speed of airplanes doubled overnight and eventually tripled. That phenomenon is about to happen in education. It is called a design breakthrough, and it is what this book is all about.

In a parallel to our discussion on principals, a new professionalism in teaching will not result simply from increased pay. As important as pay is, there must be a revolution in the preparation of teachers as well. Professionalism is about adherence to a set of best practices, not for rules' sake but out of an understanding that, until replaced with better ones, proven best practices should drive our methods. Professionalism is a belief that as important as art and creativity are, science matters, too. It is about strict protocols. It's about a real body of knowledge that must be learned if one is to be a true member of the profession. It comes through years of study and years of work side by side with those who know this.

Schools of the future will look to two key improvements in the education of teachers to move professionalism of teachers to a new level:

First, schools of the future will incorporate the residency concept of medicine, the associate concept of law, the assistant-professor concept of universities, the apprentice idea employed in the arts. The right to be called "teacher" will come once you have truly been taught, the right to instruct once you have been instructed. And that occurs best when you have been side by side with teachers in a school. Just as medicine has teaching hospitals, schools of the future will build in development of their teaching force.

Second, we need a revolution in our colleges of education. There are great schools of education out there, just as there are great public schools out there. But if we are to move to a new school design, there must be a corresponding evolution in the design of our colleges of education.

Let's discuss both in more detail.

The Teacher Intern

There is a growing recognition that brand-new teachers need additional support. This recognition has been fueled by the large number of teachers who leave the field within two or three years of their arrival. Many school systems now provide those young teachers extra and specialized professional development. And many individual schools attempt to provide them with various types of support, such as mentoring by more experienced teachers. Although well intended, these efforts typically are ad hoc, poorly funded, and, relative to the needs of these new teachers, half measures. For the most part, America's beginning teachers

are thrown, on their own, into the frontline trenches of education, spending most of their days alone with their students, alone
with their stresses and struggles. And because union agreements
allow experienced teachers the right to choose the best schools,
many, even most, of America's beginning teachers are thrown
right into the cauldrons of educational crises, the toughest, most
challenging classrooms in America. It would be as if the U.S.
Army assigned its least experienced battalions to the most challenging battles. The results would be as they are in thousands of
urban schools: World War I–like casualty rates for teachers and
students alike.

Schools of the future will not tolerate this. Beginning teachers
will be intern teachers. And they'll be given the support they absolutely require to become teachers. That support will come in
one key way: they will learn at the side of a master, just as a co-
pilot learns from his captain, just as an associate learns from a
senior law partner, just as an intern learns from his attending
physician in what is known in hospitals as grand rounds. It will be
done elbow to elbow, with lead and senior teachers spending real
time, every week, in the interns' classrooms. But to do this, lead
and senior teachers must be relieved of substantial amounts of
time from their classes, trained to be effective coaches and devel-
opers, and given a certain authority to direct and correct. These
are design "specs" that schools of the future will incorporate. They
will be critical parts of the development of a true faculty—not
add-ons.

New Teacher Colleges

As radical new school designs come into being in the decades
ahead, their counterparts should be launched in colleges of edu-

cation. To lead the way in that revolution, America should launch ten new teacher colleges. The objective would not be to replace current teacher colleges but rather to provide several significant examples of what teacher education should be in the future.

Again, as in the principal universities described above, the federal government can play an important role in jump-starting this effort. The last section of this book will show in detail how it can occur.

What, you might ask, are the big differences between what we see today in schools of education and some of these new designs? Five things come to mind.

First, I hope we will see far more rigorous courses on "performance-oriented teaching"—the setting of annual educational goals for individual children, real-time assessment of progress, the monitoring of data that demonstrates progress on a child-by-child basis, and finally, the tactics for adjusting instruction when impediments are discovered. If school cultures are to be transformed into "we must deliver" organizations, then teachers need a head start on that mindset long before they arrive at the school.

Second, I discussed earlier how schools must move toward a design that incorporates much more independent learning. This is a crucial element in schools of the future. For this to happen, teachers must become adept at myriad tasks related to independent learning. They must become coaches and facilitators as much as lecturers, floating seamlessly from "station" to "station," student to student, strand to strand, project to project—launching a project here, nudging one along there, and stopping one that is going nowhere. Beginning teachers should not be left to figure this out on their own.

Third, teachers of the future must have a very high degree of computer literacy and, in particular, great skill in the navigation of assessment systems that will provide crucial data about their students. Just as any MBA is a master of Excel, so must teachers know how to manipulate expertly the real-time assessment systems that will be coming to market.

Fourth, these new colleges should acquaint aspiring teachers with new school designs, particularly with how school staff will be differently organized. What are the roles and responsibilities of lead teachers in these new types of organizations? How should beginning teachers utilize these new resources in their intern years? How do teachers rise through these new types of structures? Such courses will enable our teachers to arrive at their first schools well prepared to deal with designs that are a far cry from what they experienced during their own K–12 days.

Finally, too often teachers are taught at a great distance from the front lines of school—particularly, far away from the realities they will confront in many urban schools. Future teacher colleges will increase the amount of "live fire training" like that seen in the military.

CHAPTER 7

Beyond Students and Staff

Schools with 100 Percent Guarantees

As a young man, I was once walking through Greenwich Village in New York City. Sprawled on the sidewalk in front of me was a disheveled man lying facedown. He was probably drunk or drugged, who knew. But what I do know is this: I did not reach down to help, despite my conscience saying loudly that I should. Instead, along with hundreds of others on that busy street, I walked right on by. In the small town in Tennessee where I grew up, this would have been an unthinkable act, but here it was accepted. As I walked along the street, looking back, I was shocked by my own indifference. I said to myself, "How can you do this!" I swore then and there that I would never do it again. But I did, and more than once.

It was, upon reflection, a certain loss of innocence, a lowering of standards, a very slippery slope, a road to "Well, I guess that's just the way it is. There's just so much we can do." Such adjustments happen in many aspects of life. And unfortunately, such has happened in our schools. To take nothing away from the selfless efforts of millions who work within our schools every day, as a nation we have come to accept that failure is an option, that it is "just the way it is," that it is somehow okay that tens of thousands of our schools don't work for the children within them, that illiteracy is, call it what you will, "acceptable" for a few million children and families in our society. As Chapter 1 conveyed, we have hundreds of schools in America where almost no children are achieving proficiency. We have thousands of schools where 70 percent and more of children are functioning below basic literacy levels. As a nation, we are "walking by" these children. We are no longer stopping. We are no longer shocked. We are no longer outraged.

Schools of the future will have an embedded culture of outrage, a genetic commitment to accountability, and a mentality that believes and requires, with rare exception, *that all children should achieve significant levels of proficiency in reading, math, and other basic skills.* The No Child Left Behind Act has stated this, and it is a good starting point. But schools must "operationalize" this ethos, making it an integral part of their culture. There must be a built-in view that it is not acceptable for children to fail. These schools will know that a failing test score by a child is also one earned by the school, that learning and teaching are simultaneously assessed. In schools of the future, leadership will *assume* highly consistent academic results the same way flight crews assume flawless performance, the same way doctors and patients now expect near perfection in certain basic procedures. In hospitals and airplanes, lives are on the line. In schools, the quality of those lives is determined. The standards should be the same.

We give lip service to this type of "no excuses" and "100 percent guaranteed" culture today, but it is more a political statement than a genetic code of school operations. The federal NCLB law says all schools will have 100 percent of their children proficient in reading and math by the year 2014. Legislatively, it is clearly the right objective, the right direction, and it is having an impact. But legislation, in and of itself, doesn't change the *operating culture* of a school. It just exposes deficiency and, one would hope, causes schools to think about what they must do to solve the problem. And education law does that only if it is rigorously enforced, which, unfortunately, in many cases it is not. Too often, the consequence for school failure is no more than "house arrest" or "Here, try again with more money." Or too often, the unachieved standards themselves are changed. Government transforms failure simply by describing it otherwise. The only way school culture really gets transformed is through explicit, inculcated "design measures."

How will that happen? Cultures come from values constantly and compellingly conveyed through powerful, conscious systems. These are meant not only to convey information but also to create common bonds, common belief systems. Ask the Marine Corps. Ask Dell. Ask the Post Office fifty years ago. Ask Federal Express today. If you saw the movie *Cast Away,* perhaps you remember the opening scene, in which the character played by Tom Hanks attempts to "export" the FedEx culture on the importance of time to workers at the FedEx facility in Moscow. That's commitment to a culture! Schools of the future will have it. One hundred percent reliability will not be a saying, it will be a religion, and in no small part, that ethos will deliver the day, just as FedEx's delivery folks do.

To establish this, schools of the future must communicate this new culture constantly and at every opportunity. The message begins in the recruitment of both principals and teachers. Just as the Marines begin to create their culture in recruitment—the now politically incorrect "A Few Good Men"—so it will be with schools of the future. New teachers and principals will be asked, "Do you want to be a part of a 100-percent-guaranteed culture? Are you up to the task of that kind of commitment? If not, you might want to choose another school." And then, from their first day of orientation and throughout their entire experience at the school, this code will be emphasized, again and again. Schools of the future will refine and hone this communication. It will be their national anthem, their "Just do it" mantra.

But as critical as communication is, it is only the context for achievement, not achievement itself. In the Marines, the message is effectively "We shall always prevail." The Marine Corps then makes that message real by providing Marines with the tactics, the support, and the weapons that they need in order to prevail. A message without backup actually breeds the undertow of culture: cynicism. It is a virus that has swept America's schools. Teachers have seen leaders with their messages come and go so often with little to support them. Schools of the future will not make that mistake.

The Wired and Wireless School

American schools have made a hash of technology. Literally billions have gone down the toilet as schools have struggled to integrate the computer into day-to-day education. I say this from experience: Edison Schools, perhaps the most technologically advanced system of schools in the United States today, has often made mistakes in this arena.

But tremendous news is just on the horizon. While the computer and K–12 education have barely met, they are about to be married, and their marriage will be a central driver in school designs of the decade ahead. Computers have recently evolved in ways that make them even more applicable to schools and instruction than they were before. They're much more powerful than a decade ago in speed and memory, which radically alters what they can do for students and teachers; broadband has made communication between them so much easier; and cost, a huge, almost defining impediment to widespread use in the past, has fallen to a point where school designs of the future now can find the funds.

Let's skip what went wrong and what went right with computer use in schools in years past other than to make one general point: In business settings, computers, networks, and applications (both off the shelf and discretely developed) have become critical to entire enterprises. In large numbers of companies, particularly those that are "information rich," *everyone* has a computer and *everyone* relies on the network and the applications that are provided by the organization. Many companies literally could not function without their technology backbones. This infrastructure is considered to be as critical as air and light. Though schools have begun to deploy computers more and more, especially in connecting schools to their district offices, computers are not a critical aspect of what goes on in a classroom on a day-to-day basis. There are numerous telling signs of this. In many schools not all teachers have their own personal computers; in the vast majority of schools, students are not provided their own computers; and people at thousands of schools can relate frequent stories of in-the-school networks that are down for days and weeks at a time—hardly an indication that technology is a critical factor in instruction.

This is about to change. In schools of the future, computer ubiquity and computer reliability will equal what we see in most modern business enterprises. And this will not come about because of a mindless fascination with computers, but because computers, networks, and applications will be critical to the new school designs. What is exciting is that none of this is Buck Rogers speculation, as it would have been a decade ago. It's all in the here and now, even in a few hundred of the nation's most advanced schools, primarily in "pilot" mode.

School designs of the future will all incorporate similar hardware, network, and application packages, with these six key components:

1. A laptop for every teacher, issued and maintained by the school.
2. A laptop for every student (beginning in the third grade), to be issued and maintained by the school, complete with a padded backpack for going back and forth between home and school.
3. Wireless network capability throughout the school.
4. Networks that are maintained with the same level of urgency and care that we see in American businesses.
5. A suite of software applications, including old standbys like the Microsoft Office suite but also including specially designed applications such as a monthly assessment system for all students; electronic report cards; and a significant amount of curriculum online.

All the above exists here and there in individual schools, but no school system in the United States begins to approach this capability.

What, you might ask, does an infrastructure like this cost? About $400 per student per year, assuming you amortize the cost over the useful life of the equipment or, as most school systems will probably do, simply lease it. That's about two times the current technological investment of many U.S. schools and about 4.6 percent of the $8,742 per pupil we now spend every year. This could be funded from increased investment in education or by eliminating other, less valuable investments. That will be discussed later in this chapter.

This technology package is not an end, but rather a means to achieving a critical aspect of the new designs of the future. Without highways, cars would not be what they are today. Similarly, without highly developed technological infrastructure, schools will not be able to make the leap to achieving meaningful levels of independent learning.

Life Skills

Reading, writing, arithmetic, and a few other core subjects in the standard American school curriculum are must-haves to succeed in modern-day life. But today's curriculum leaves out, or does not sufficiently emphasize, many core skills that would also help our children excel after school. No longer. Schools of the future will include a rich core-skills curriculum that provides graduating students with a set of practical capabilities useful in any career or field. What will that new curriculum include?

As noted in our discussion of student motivation, the number-one addition will be a course on what a person does after school, called Careers and Jobs. If they were asked to name ten careers (excluding doctors and lawyers), most students today would be hard-pressed to do so. And why would they know? Most children of professionals, for example, will probably know where their parents work, but they might have little knowledge of what they actually do. I am as guilty of this as the next parent. My children know that I am the CEO of a company that runs schools, but I've never tried to explain to them what a CEO does or how I arrived at that role.

Another important module will be a broad and deep course on the use of technology, mainly the computer and its relative, the Internet. Though schools are generally touching on this now, few do it in the depth it deserves. In some respects, the forerunner of this technology class was the typing class. When I look back on my high school days, I view that course as one of the most useful. Somehow I learned to type at 100 words a minute—and I think of the countless hours that course has saved me. For sure, keyboarding will be one of the core-skills classes, but it will be just one in a suite of practical courses on technology. Students should graduate these days with complete proficiency and literacy in all major computer applications. They should be as fluent in the language of technology (today it's Word, Power-Point, Excel, and Outlook or other branded substitutes) as they are in English. These programs are the pencils, slide rules, chalkboards, and palettes of modern times, and our curricula must incorporate them. Beyond the major applications, students need a working knowledge of the operating systems that run those applications. Though it might be acceptable that many of us are oblivious to what actually happens under the hood of a car, that cannot be the case with a tool so central for the centuries ahead. Finally, there is the Internet itself. It is our new, vast library in the sky. We must teach our students how to navigate it with ease.

Some might say that students are doing just fine learning all of the above on their own. Though they are ahead of their parents, for sure, there *is* a difference between just picking something up and knowing it very well. Hunting and pecking at 50 words a minute isn't bad, but it is just half as good as 100 words a minute. Understanding 30 percent of the functionality of Excel will probably get you through, but anyone who has seen the speed and efficiency of someone who really knows its ins and outs appreciates that true proficiency is a far different level and will result in higher levels of success.

But life skills do not end at technology. Mental and physical health is another area schools should address in both different and more complete ways. The "health class" has been around for decades. We all remember the food groups (or do we?). But did anyone really teach the true application of that information to diet? Did anyone show us how to design our own diet in workable ways, so that we could really understand the number of calories required to maintain or lose weight? Do school cafeterias serve food with calorie counts displayed? Both health class and its close relative, physical education, suffer from a disconnect to the future of the student: how we should really use this information to be healthier. The current level of childhood obesity indicates that these classes should be issuing a lot of failing grades. Push-ups and chinning have been mainstays of PE classes, but how often does anyone actually show students how to develop a personal workout regimen and teach them the importance of that? Speaking of independent learning, is it not sensible that high school students be responsible for their own workouts— again not in class? And what of substance abuse? Could we talk more in our schools about why students are drawn to drugs, what really happens out there on the street, and what they should do when things go wrong?

Moreover, health classes have largely omitted the health of the mind. Introducing any significant degree of psycho-dynamic knowledge at the K–12 level would likely result in educational wars akin to those over the distribution of condoms—but would it not help to introduce a degree of "self-awareness" information to youngsters, enough that they might have a working knowledge of the basic ailments of the psyche that afflict most of us at one time or another in our lives?

And then there is money. For a culture maligned for its focus on money, we do a remarkable job of hiding information about it from our children. Is it no wonder that parents criticize their children's fiscal irresponsibility? How could we expect our youth to be anything but irresponsible, given the way we keep them in the dark about money? Most students have little idea what their parents make, what any particular career pays, or what it costs to live in a particular way. How unseemly! Living in the drought of economic information they live in, students often view economic success as a kind of lottery, where maybe someone scores big in the NBA or someone makes a killing on Wall Street, each quickly and without great effort. A practical course on money would send our children into the world better prepared.

While many schools have public speaking classes, how many have "presentation courses," where students are taught the equivalent of the instant messaging of the business and professional world? And do we really teach children time management, the art of scheduling and keeping a calendar, and the simple rules about how to keep a good to-do list?

We don't. We should. And we will.

Early Concentration of Force
and the Third-Grade Diploma

In a meeting with a large urban school system about the possibility of Edison's managing some failing schools, the superintendent informed me that the elementary and middle schools were doing well, but the high schools were a mess. He offered up the idea of having Edison manage twenty high schools. I declined. Children don't just suddenly fall off a learning cliff. I knew that the elementary schools and middle schools probably weren't that good—they just felt that way. Discipline is not nearly as difficult at elementary schools, where the inherent cuteness of children masks the reality of what is going on.

As an example of this, we were once asked to manage an elementary school in which 99 percent of the children were failing (as Chapter 1 showed, that horrific state of affairs is more common than we allow ourselves to realize). We decided to dismiss the principal of the school, largely on the basis that he had served there for many years with no improvement in student performance. On an achievement basis, the school was flatlining. We were stunned when the *parents* of the schoolchildren protested our move, literally demanding a hearing on the atrocity of his dismissal! It turned out that while the principal did little as far as achievement was concerned, he was much beloved by both parents and students. The school was a warm and safe place, albeit an illiterate one.

A great elementary education is a must in our society, and it is *then* that we must establish core literacy and numeric proficiency. Though children can be "saved" at later dates, the chances of doing so dramatically decline—and the costs dramatically rise. So we must succeed early with our children.

Some cities are dealing with this through "holding kids back"—ending social promotion. Though this is arguably a move in the right direction (why should we send them to higher grades where they will inevitably fail and where their frustration will inevitably increase?), it should also be noted that we are holding them back to be supposedly reeducated by the very institution that failed them in the first place. And the trauma of being held back is undeniable, a blow to children's self-esteem that cannot be simply argued away. It is punishing them for the failure of the institution that is supposed to be serving them.

Our schools should make sure, through every method possible, that *all* children are at proficiency by a certain point in the elementary experience—probably at the end of third or fourth grade. Rather than take the extreme measure of holding students back at a certain grade, we should help them out all along the way. Just as "lack of proficiency" does not occur at a certain date, neither does successful intervention. Children fall behind gradually, across months and years. Our schools should not wake up at grade three and say, "Oh my God, our children can't read and therefore we need to hold them back." We should have (and already do have) assessment techniques that provide early warning signs of failure. We should deal with learning problems in increments, just as they arise.

The concept of "concentration of forces"—which simply means that as a child falls behind in literacy and numeracy, we increase the amount of time spent with that child on those competencies—will be a core strategy used by schools of the future. To make the point, imagine that you are a student midway through the second grade and that your reading assessment shows you are not even approaching the level of reading skills that you should have. Also imagine that you have a seven-hour school day and are spending sixty minutes of that on reading, only 14 percent. A good 86 percent of the day is spent on mathematics, art, PE, some early social studies, music—all important, but all of which you *will* fail in later grades because of your lack of reading skills. Reading is the gateway to all other subjects, the building block of all future learning. Fail it and you *will* fail everything else, except perhaps music and sports. Why, then, is the school not taking virtually *all* of your day to ensure your proficiency in reading? Reason: We just don't do it that way. We adhere to a design that is as rigid, in educational terms, as the military tactics in World War I, where we sent troops again and again across an open field in the face of withering machine-gun fire. Some more advanced schools do shift more resources to reading. One program (used by Edison) called "Success for All" demands that a participating school increase the reading time for students to ninety minutes *at the beginning of the day,* when students are most ready to learn (and teachers most ready to teach). This is absolutely the right direction, but when students are not making it, we need to move faster.

Our objective should be a "third-grade diploma" that signals a student has achieved a certain proficiency in both reading and math. Every school's objective should be that virtually 100 percent of students receive this diploma. Our plan should be to send them on, not to hold them back.

Another important aspect of an earlier concentration of forces is a reversal of our thinking about how we invest in our schools. As a nation, we increase spending as children come of age. *We should do the reverse*—and schools of the future will do so.

Our current practice has simply grown up around us. The theory for why it should be as it is (and "theory" is probably a kind word to apply given the absence of public debate on the subject) would probably go something like this: Subject matter becomes more complex and varied, and therefore costs increase. In fact, if you study how money is spent for higher grades, you find that a large percentage goes to remedial education, spending directly related to the failure of earlier grades. The question is: What portion of special education students truly require that expenditure, and what portion are students who were not well served during their "foundation years"? They—and we—would have been better served by a higher investment in earlier grades *and* an extension of public efforts below kindergarten, the earliest grade that most states fund.

One way to think about this reversal in investment strategy is to look at how spending per child might be allocated differently. America currently provides its children with twelve or thirteen years of education, K–12. (There is some minor spending below that, but let's leave it out here for the sake of simplicity.) We invest approximately $114,000 per child for these thirteen years, $8,742 per year. Policy makers, modelers, and school designers should consider the effect of "weighting" this spending differently across the years. If we do a good job in our lower grades, two things will happen to decrease the cost of the higher grades. First, students will become increasingly independent in their learning capacity, and will require less adult supervision. Second, class sizes will actually rise.

More-on-Warhead, Less-on-Delivery System

During World War II, Russian commanders, short on arms, sometimes sent troops into battle without weapons. Soldiers were told to simply pick them up from fallen comrades. Though we don't send teachers into classrooms with nothing, we certainly send them far less equipped than we might. Consider this: America spends $138 billion a year on teacher salaries but only $10.4 billion a year on the curriculum teachers use, their "educational weaponry"—a people-to-program ratio of 13 to 1. It is as if we had built an Atlas rocket (the delivery system) and then placed a BB (the warhead) on top of it. Compare the difference of approach in our military, where an Air Force pilot's "weapon" may be a $180 million F-22.

The result is twofold: (1) we ask the impossible of teachers, and (2) we bore children to tears. We ask the impossible of teachers because we provide them with textbooks that would put dead people to sleep, and then ask them, day in and day out, to inspire, engage, and involve their students. We bore students because that is simply too much to ask of our teachers, and the students inevitably fail.

The mantra in schooling over the past few decades has been to increase the number of teachers and pay them more. That is half right—the pay part. What we should add is that they must be equipped with the best, most exciting curriculum possible.

Reality-Testing the Cost
of New School Designs

Everything that has been recommended in the past three chapters on school design can be done probably for what we currently spend on schools, assuming a new school design includes everything that we have discussed—both the additional costs and the cost-saving opportunities. It would be much easier to do (and better) if schools had an additional 10 percent of funding, and as a nation we should try to get them that, but we should not let the lack of that increment stand in the way of a revolution in school design.

Some of my recommendations require additional dollars, some are neutral, and others actually save money. Those that require dollars are increasing pay for principals, significantly ramping up spending on more advanced curriculum materials and programming, and significantly improving the technology infrastructure. Those that are neutral or largely neutral are a culture of accountability, substantially increasing teacher pay (if we correspondingly decrease the number of teachers), adding a "life skills" curriculum, and shifting spending from higher grades to earlier grades. The two that actually save money are more independent learning, which reduces the number of teachers needed, and the "student chores" program, which alleviates a variety of costs, particularly a portion of in-school tutoring and administrative and operational costs.

Saying all this is one thing and doing it is another, and therefore it is instructive (and confidence-building, for those of us who actually would like to see these designs come into being) to compare a typical school budget with the potential budget for a school of the future. Below is a snapshot comparing a K–8 school that has a total of 900 students, with 100 students in each grade, and the national average spending of $8,742 per student under today's typical design with such a school under a future design in a larger system of schools. This was not done on an envelope but actually was run through a financial modeling system that Edison has used for hundreds of school budgets over the past decade. The comparison is presented here in a highly summarized form:

CURRENT AND FUTURE SCHOOL BUDGET		
	CURRENT DESIGN	FUTURE DESIGN
Principal	$80,000	$160,000
Teachers	$2,760,000 (60 teachers X $46,000 per)	$2,800,000 (40 teachers X $70,000 per)
Student Chores	$0 (0 FTEs*)	$100,000 (67.5 FTEs*)
Total FTEs	60	107.5
Curriculum	$200,000	$600,000
Technology	$150,000	$300,000
Other	$2,710,850	$2,334,240
System support	$1,966,950	$1,573,560
Total	$7,867,800	$7,867,800

*FTEs = full-time equivalent teachers and "chore" providers

The chart shows a *very* different school design from the one that America now has. It doubles the cash compensation of a school leader. It increases average teacher pay by over 50 percent and the highest teacher pay by 100 percent. The new design triples a school's investment in curriculum to make the materials much more exciting. It doubles the robustness of current school technology platforms and moves schools to the wireless systems they need. And it actually increases the FTEs (full-time equivalent staff) of a school by 67.5 people, mainly by letting students help run the school. The cost increases are funded by reducing the overall number of teachers—through increased independent learning, better technology use, and assistance from students themselves. (Note: No current teacher in America would be laid off, as any move to a model like this could be easily handled through annual teacher attrition.) Additionally, this new model reduces the amount of general and administrative expense through scale, by greatly enlarging the size of overall school systems. According to the U.S. Department of Education, the current average G&A load of a school is 25 percent of its spending. That is not surprising, as the average school system in the United States has only six schools. The model presented above assumes the existence of a larger system of schools, the road to which I'll discuss in Chapter 8, and uses this larger scale to reduce the G&A load to 20 percent.

What the chart shows is that *this can be done.* The biggest push is, of course, in reducing the total number of teachers in order that we can pay teachers much more. Many might ask, "Is it realistic to run a school of 900 students with 40 teachers?" It isn't if you think of schools in the "old way," where students are always in class, where students are not doing any of the work of running a school, and where student motivation is rather low. But if you change those assumptions—if you assume that students can do a lot on their own, that students can manage some of the school, that students care deeply about their own education, and that schools are no longer organized in tiny cottage-industry scale— then school could be a very different place, a very different place indeed.

And a much more effective one.

CHAPTER 8

School Systems
and School Companies
in 2030

To take America's schools to a new level of performance, we must radically change not only schools but also the systems and structures that surround and support them. These new systems will, in large part, bring about the changes in school design discussed in the previous three chapters. This chapter focuses on what school systems and schooling companies of the future will be if we are to bring about a new and better generation of schools.

The date 2030 is not chosen casually. What I am about to describe can easily happen within that span of time. Just as goals to eradicate certain diseases by a particular date or to land a man on the moon were successfully achieved, so America can eradicate failing schools by 2030. Illiteracy or near illiteracy, a condition we nationally inflict upon nearly 30 percent of our children, can be, for all practical purposes, a memory, not a reality. The national disgrace of an achievement gap between poor and rich, black or brown and white, can be a thing of the past. Indeed, our public school system can be the finest on the globe—sustaining our global leadership rather than threatening it. K–12 education, in fact, could become an important U.S. *export,* just as our higher-education system is. This is within our grasp as a nation within the next twenty-five years, if, as the final chapter in this book urges, our political and educational leaders exercise their vision, power, and skills of persuasion.

Some will undoubtedly say that achieving the kind of profound systemic change I will describe is a bridge too far, something not achievable within a couple of decades, if ever. It is instructive, then, to look at other sectors to see what can happen in a twenty-five-year span of time.

Let us start with the automotive world. In 1959, import cars represented 1 percent of new car sales in the United States. In 1965, the president of Nissan America reportedly walked around selling cars door to door in Southern California. Hondas were viewed as cheap tin toys, not serious cars. By 1975, imports accounted for 21 percent of the U.S. auto market, and by 1989, import sales had soared to 33 percent of U.S. automotive sales. Why? Superior design prevailed with consumers.

Let's move to computers. Today around 60 percent of all households in the United States have at least one personal computer. Millions of homes have a personal computer for *every* person in the home. We don't just take computers for granted; we cannot imagine life without them. Computer companies that are now giants were not in people's imaginations twenty-five years ago. Dell, founded in 1984, today is a $49 billion-per-year behemoth employing over 55,000 people.

Then there's the Internet. Just twenty years ago, few people other than researchers at scientific institutions and in the defense industry had even heard of it. E-mail was limited to a tiny few.

Asked what a search engine was, people might think of a rescue vehicle. Asked to explain a website, they might say, "Home of a spider?" Google, Amazon, and AOL did not exist. You could not design your sneakers online. You would not have known what on-line was. The entire world of virtual commerce might have been found in a science fiction book.

And what about overnight delivery? In 1965, Federal Express was an idea in a term paper at Yale (for which Fred Smith, the soon-to-become founder, received a C—forever proving that grading or assessment is not infallible). By 1990, twenty-five years later, overnight delivery to virtually anywhere in the world was commonplace. If you want to see what can happen in such a short span of time, visit FedEx's Memphis hub, where every night for as far as the eye can see jumbo jets are lined up on approach two abreast, bearing freight, documents, and, perhaps, term papers on their way to a less-than-visionary professor.

The point is that in other sectors of our life and economy, twenty-five years is a *transforming* period of time, a period in which the magical and unimaginable can occur. That can happen in education as well. We have been unintentionally trained to expect otherwise by the glacial rate of change in our schools during the past century. But no immutable law requires it to be so.

So if we suspend our disbelief, if we apply the dynamics and rates of change commonplace in other arenas, if we think, as other industries do, that transformation is a prerequisite to survival, what could our school systems (and the companies that will serve them) look like in 2030?

Let's imagine the reality of two school systems and one schooling company in that year—and also imagine some of the events along the way. Of America's nearly 15,000 school districts, I've chosen two: New York, New York, and the fictitious Middleburg, Tennessee. I've selected them for this futuristic journey because they capture the range of school systems in America today.

New York City is now my home. The New York City public schools are America's largest system of schools, 1,200 of them, with over 1 million students and an annual operating budget of $12 billion. It is one of only twenty-five school districts in America with an enrollment of over 100,000 students. Seventy-three percent of its children are impoverished. Eighty-five percent are children of color.

Middleburg is like where I grew up, and there are thousands of districts that are very similar. It has just fifteen schools, twelve thousand students, and an annual budget of $96 million. Eighty percent of its students are white.

The two districts are 700 miles apart, literally and figuratively. Yet if I am right about the future, each will see changes in the next two and half decades that will dwarf any from the previous hundred years.

Grawson Schools, the schooling company that I portray, does not exist. It is completely fictitious. I've imagined that it grew from an equally fictitious large K–12 publisher.

So let's jump ahead twenty-five years and imagine that we are looking back. The characters are not real. So as not to confuse the reader, the statistics and numbers used in 2030 (such as enrollments, revenues, per-pupil spending, etc.) are the most current statistic.

New York City, 2030

New York City schools chancellor Laverne Chub knows she is headed for her first major crisis. She's happy with the performance of four of her five schooling companies: Horizon Schools; Grawson Schools; her only import, Mandela Academies; and, somewhat reluctantly, Franklin Schools. (Chub, sixty-three, an education veteran, still has a bit of lingering attitude toward Franklin, a remnant of "the roaring teens," as schooling pioneers describe the period from 2010 to 2020, when Franklin had the schooling category pretty much to itself and a swagger to match. Chub puts up with it, given the company's overall performance.) But Schools for Children, an L.A.-based entity, continues to fall behind its competition in the recently released *Consumer Reports* EdWatch data that ranks the performance of the city's five school providers for New York City parents. When Chub looks at the following chart, the conclusion is obvious:

COMPARATIVE ACHIEVEMENT PERFORMANCE				
	% PROFICIENT	% ADVANCED	COMBINED % PROFICIENT AND ADVANCED	ANNUAL RATE OF GAIN IN ADVANCED
Mandela Academies	50%	38%	88%	3.2 points
Franklin Schools	52%	35%	87%	2.8 points
Horizon Schools	53%	32%	85%	2.5 points
Grawson Schools	55%	29%	84%	2.2 points
Schools for Children	57%	22%	79%	1.2 points

Schools for Children is a full 16 points below Mandela in getting children to the advanced category on state assessments. More important, its rate of gain in that category continues to lag behind all its competitors'. Chub has endured this lag for three years, and she is convinced it is time to exercise the termination clause in Schools for Children's 160-school, $1.6 billion annual contract. It is going to be a major fight—and one she might lose. But a bit of history can help one understand Chub's plight.

In 2017 New York City entered into twenty-year contracts with each of the five companies noted above to manage, collectively, 1,000 of the city's schools. The largest contract was for 270 schools, with Grawson Schools; the smallest was with Horizon, a relative newcomer, which was awarded 50 schools. Originally, as some other cities had done in an effort to appease various constituencies and to maintain some core capabilities in case things did not work out, New York City continued to manage 200 schools itself. Based on achievement results and a growing comfort with this new approach, however, the district discontinued direct operation of its own sites in 2025, transferring day-to-day management of the remaining 200 schools to the five companies.

Though it managed the largest multiprovider contracting effort in U.S. education history, New York was, in fact, late to the party. Philadelphia, following its pioneering efforts begun in 2002, had moved completely to this approach by 2013. Philadelphia had begun with a concept called "thin management," in which providers had responsibility for only educational aspects of schools. Once that approach proved its merits, Philadelphia—and many other cities that had followed in its tracks—moved to a more comprehensive plan. (Paul Vallas, the pioneering head of the Philadelphia system, had said to MSNBC in December 2004 that he thought half of Philadelphia's schools might be in some form of private management by 2009. His vision was very close to correct.) Of the top fifty cities in the United States, New York City was the forty-fifth to move completely to the multiprovider model. Two events finally broke the logjam. Most important, the longtime chief of the United Federation of Teachers, Randi Weingarten, lobbied strongly for the move, concluding, after watching achievement surge in Philly and other AFT multiprovider cities, that it would greatly enhance the well-being of not only children in New York but teacher members as well. (It didn't hurt that the AFT had also forged "national understandings" with all five of the winning entities.) The second precipitating event was the New York State legislature's passage of a special funding measure that helped New York City transition its large central office, a move many states had used to entice large systems to adopt this new model.

The contracts New York negotiated with each company were different in size but similar in many other respects. Each company had complete management responsibility for its schools, including curriculum, instruction, finances, cleaning, food, and enrollment. No company was allowed to choose children. If a school had more applications than spaces, it was required to admit students through a lottery. Each company had substantial incentives and penalties tied to student achievement. Though the contracts were twenty years in length, they could be terminated if a company failed over any three-year period to reach achievement targets (which is why Chub was planning to terminate Schools for Children).

The school district maintained all the key overarching system-management responsibilities. First and foremost, it had responsibility for hiring, monitoring, and, if necessary, firing the five companies. Second, in partnership with the state, it controlled the "high stakes" assessment of children in order to watch carefully how each company was doing. Third, all funds flowed through it to the companies. The district kept 1 percent of state, federal, and local operating funds as a "monitoring and quality-control" fee, passing the other 99 percent on to the schools and their five providers. This concept had been adopted as an industry standard across the country. Fourth, through its capital budget the district owned, constructed, and renovated all school facilities, though the companies were responsible for cleaning and minor repairs. Fifth, it received and followed up on any complaints from parents. Sixth, all teachers remained under a collective-bargaining agreement with the district, one that allowed for the five different formats. The district remained responsible for the periodic negotiation of this agreement, with input and consultation from the five providers. Last, while individual schools chose their staff members, staff were joint employees of the district and the provider, allowing them to remain in state retirement systems.

The district left day-to-day operation of the schools to the companies. As a result, the district office—those individuals not housed in a school—which had numbered in the thousands (the number depending on whose propaganda one believed) at its height in 2012, now numbered 500, with the largest group a state-of-the-art online "call center" of 200 that fielded complaints from citizens. While the district office had shrunk, many individuals formerly part of district administration had migrated to positions with the provider companies, each of which had built significant regional facilities to manage its portfolio of schools. Franklin has a "New York Regional HQ" of over 500 full-time central staff members dedicated to the 240 New York City schools it manages. And that regional office is substantially supported by Franklin's national and global HQ. If you add up the regional HQs of the five companies, however, they still equal only half the old district office.

Though late in adopting this new approach, New York handled the five contracts in some innovative ways. Some cities required individual companies to manage all the schools within a geographic section of the city. Example: In Los Angeles, Franklin managed all the schools in Watts, while Horizon was responsible for everything in the North Hollywood area. But New York demanded that each company have some of its schools in *each* neighborhood. This had two significant results. First, citizens had three or four very different types of schools to choose from in, or within reach of, their neighborhood, giving them *real school choice, but without the ideological (and, to some, highly distracting) wars of a voucher plan.* Parents could choose any nearby school they desired. The knowledge that its students could walk down the street to a competitor at any time placed even more pressure on each company to provide excellent service.

Though Chub is unhappy with Schools for Children, she knows that the overall plan has worked, and remarkably so. New York City experienced significant gains between 2000 and 2008 during the days of the bipartisan NCLB Act. Even after what some refer to as the NCLB Amnesty Act of 2011, the city's schools showed some progress. But by 2017, hundreds of thousands of children were still not proficient, leaving many of the city's children, mostly poor and of color, doomed to lives of partial illiteracy and almost certain economic misery). And to the embarrassment of the city, proficiency rates were a full 20 percent behind cities up and down the Eastern seaboard that had adopted the multiprovider model earlier. Since 2017, however, the five schooling organizations had moved the number of proficient or advanced from 50 percent to 85 percent. Even more dramatic, the number of children achieving advanced status had surged sixfold, meaning that hundreds of thousands of children were poised to enter highly competitive universities. Just a decade earlier they would have been headed for something very different. Indeed, as a result, the burgeoning industry of companies providing university degrees was reporting to share-holders an expected surge in the number of children entering college.

But back to Ms. Chub's problem. Why, you might ask, is firing Schools for Children such an issue? What parent would not want to upgrade to one of the higher-performing schools, particularly given their close geographic proximity? The problem was thornier than that. First, Schools for Children had an enrollment of over 180,000 children in New York City. The families of those children had all chosen Schools for Children. Many had been at a Schools for Children campus for their entire educational lives. And many of their parents (and grandparents) remembered what New York's schools used to be like. Compared with schools of the past, Schools for Children has been great. Second, with over 10,000 employees in New York City and another 4,000 through-out the state of New York, Schools for Children is a major po-litical force. Predictably, Chub has been receiving calls from politicos saying, "Do you have to fire Schools for Children? Isn't there a way to work this out?" Chub doesn't think so. Monitoring these providers and, when called for, disciplining or firing them is one of her major priorities. Indeed, she sees that as the essence of a school-system leader's job. Though she views Schools for Children managers as colleagues and partners, she is the *managing* part-ner and "the chief quality officer" of education in New York City. And Schools for Children is not making the cut. Chub also be-lieves she can offer parents in the city two better options by split-ting Schools for Children's contract between two intriguing entities—one, the leading educational provider in Japan, and the other, a subsidiary of Duke University that entered the K–12 sec-tor a decade or so earlier. If the politics gets too tough, she might leave Schools for Children with a third of their current schools, which would also appease die-hard parents.

Chub calls in her communications and procurement officers to draft the release to pull the plug on Schools for Children and start the competitive process to replace them.

Middleburg, Tennessee, 2030

Dwight Hill has been superintendent of the Middleburg district since 2001. At seventy-five, he is both the longest-serving and oldest superintendent in Tennessee, serving through a special provision made possible by the governor years back in celebration of what he had accomplished. Under Hill's leadership, Middleburg schools have been Tennessee's highest-performing in thirteen of the past twenty years. And beyond that, Hill is legendary as a pioneer in Tennessee education: in 2008, he led Middleburg to become the first district in Tennessee, and in the country, to enter into what later came to be known in the education industry as an affiliation agreement. Today, in 2030, over 12,000 of America's smaller and midsized districts have such agreements. But before I describe exactly what those are, perhaps a bit of history is in order.

Beginning in 2002 and expanding rapidly between 2005 and 2015, larger, urban school systems moved toward what became known as the multiprovider model, arrangements similar to the one described above in New York City. Big districts engaged multiple companies to manage groups of schools, with the district evolving into the public authority that monitored, hired, and fired these providers. This model spread rapidly in large districts because superior achievement results became glaringly obvious (giving political leaders the platform to call for change) and because large districts had the scale to enter into multiple, significant arrangements.

But this trend did not take hold in rural, small-town, or suburban America. Smaller districts—many of which had only one elementary school, one middle school, and one high school (or just a couple of each)—found it difficult or unworkable to divide them among different providers. And the companies themselves found it economically and operationally challenging to manage a single school or even several remote sites.

There was something tragic in this. While smaller districts were often higher-performing than larger urban ones, they were perhaps the ones most in need of the state-of-the-art systems that schooling companies were building. While large urban systems had at least some scale from which to develop support capabilities, smaller districts lacked those economies.

Enter Dwight Hill. Between 2000 and 2005, Hill had watched the emergence of major schooling entities. Unlike many of his colleagues at the time, he understood that scale was an important asset, that it brought the ability to spread the costs of quality support systems across more and more sites. He also knew that this was not going to be achieved by consolidation of districts, something that states had failed to achieve to any significant degree for decades because of acute political resistance from communities that wanted control over their schools. Finally, he understood that emerging national and global schooling companies were not going to stop developing state-of-the-art school-support systems. They were going to pour more and more dollars into developing their capabilities with every school added to their systems. And the gap between large districts, which partnered with these companies, and small "unaffiliated" districts would only grow. He feared this might lead more and more citizens into the arms of the "let's get out of public education" crowd, those who were arguing that a national voucher should be handed to every citizen. So in 2004 he began dabbling with the idea of striking up a relationship with one of these entities. He began by buying Franklin's assessment engine and some of the training programs related to it. He was so pleased with how that worked that in 2007 he went back to Franklin with a much bolder idea. As is so often the case in business, the customer got there first.

What Hill proposed to Franklin was a "complete and integrated" collaboration between Middleburg and Franklin. The way he first described it to Franklin was as an analogue to American federalism, a construct in which each part (the cities, states, and federal government) did what it was best positioned and enabled to do. In a presentation to Franklin's management team in the spring of 2007, Hill laid out his plan. It was no more than ten pages of bullet points, but it was ten pages that would change the way small and middle-sized school districts in America (and ultimately throughout the world) would function in the twenty-first century. Here, in abbreviated form, is what he suggested:

1. **Middleburg School District would be the boss. In other words, this was not privatization.** In the late twentieth century, some on the political right advocated that public education should be "shut down." Their view was simple: Spending had increased in a massive way for decades, and achievement results were flat or even declining. Their solution was equally simple: Hand every student a voucher equivalent in dollars to what the public schools were spending per child to use anywhere he or she wanted (which everyone knew probably meant a private school). Where school districts were particularly resistant to change, that vision had actually played out. In thirty cities and three states in the United States, the public still technically funded public education, but it had little to do with the provision of it anymore. (The schools in these situations were now all private, and 90 percent of them started out

as and remained nonunion.) Hill wanted nothing to do with that plan, and the vision he laid out to Franklin made that clear. Middleburg School District, a distinctly public authority, would be the boss in the relationship. It, not consumers, would hire and, if necessary, fire Franklin.

2. **Middleburg would continue to "own" its school facilities and provide core services such as maintenance, transportation, and food service.** Sometimes, real estate is king. With it often come power and influence. The Middleburg School District would continue to both own all its school facilities and be responsible for major repairs and any new construction. In addition, the district would run services where intellectual property did not bring much quality or financial advantage (such as food service and transportation), although Franklin would provide some consultation.

3. **The Middleburg District would continue as the fiduciary.** The school board would continue to control the district's budget, although it would use the financial planning and control systems provided by Franklin at both the site and central level. Further, the district would consult closely with Franklin on key financial decisions, treating Franklin as a strategic partner in the future and growth of the district.

4. **Franklin would provide twelve key services to the district, ones where scale was a key determinant of excellence.** Hill called what he wanted "an integrated suite of intellectual property."

Following is the original chart of the twelve desired services as presented by Hill (and as framed in Franklin's schooling museum):

CORE SERVICES OFFERINGS—
AN INTEGRATED SUITE OF
INTELLECTUAL PROPERTY

---

1. Board professional development (PD)/training
2. Superintendent PD/training
3. Key central staff PD/training
4. Principal recruitment & PD/training
5. Teacher recruitment & PD/training

6. School design, school organization, school scheduling
7. Achievement management systems (including data systems)
8. Core curriculum (??)

9. HR systems—particularly performance compensation
10. Financial planning systems/resource allocation

11. Certain consulting services (technology, special ed, etc.)
12. Membership in "Franklin Network"

Items 1 through 5 are all about recruitment and professional development (training). Hill's view was that these required significant investment to get right, at levels that had to be spread across hundreds or even thousands of sites—something his district would never be able to achieve, given its legislatively set boundaries of operation. For example, in the area of training, how could the district really help Hill *himself* develop his skills and expertise? By definition, he was the *only* superintendent in the district. Did it really make sense for the board to create, from scratch, a training program for *one person*? The same logic was true for dozens of other leadership positions in the district. Middleburg had one head of special ed, two heads of curriculum and instruction, twelve principals, twenty art teachers, and on and on.

The same phenomenon held true in recruitment. The district typically recruited a single principal every year or so. How was it supposed to become a recruiting expert with such low frequency? Franklin, by contrast, even as early as 2005, recruited forty principals *every* year. It was well on its way to developing a significant expertise in identifying individuals who would make great school leaders. And Hill had the vision to know this would only get better and better as Franklin and other companies like it grew.

While Items 1 through 5 impacted both the district's central office and its sites, Items 6 through 8 were school-specific. Hill knew that Franklin had a highly developed school organization with thoughtfully defined roles and responsibilities for every member of a school team. There were regimens and protocols for each role that had been refined across hundreds of schools and over a decade of continuous R&D. It simply was not realistic that Middleburg or any other district of similar size was going to replicate this type of design superiority. Effectively, Middleburg would import Franklin's school design. And Middleburg would continue to use Franklin's achievement management system, which Hill had already been using. The achievement management system was the academic goal-setting, monitoring, and real-time assessment process that Franklin had spent tens of millions to perfect and keep current.

What puzzled Hill was the matter of core curriculum. In his initial presentation to Franklin, he highlighted this by placing question marks next to it. The district had its own reading, math, science, and other core-curriculum programs, purchased from various publishers. (In fact, every school had many different programs—there was no standard curriculum.) Similarly, Franklin had its own programs, some bought from publishers and, increasingly, some it had actually created. And many of Franklin's teacher professional-development programs were designed around these curriculum choices. Hill's question was whether Middleburg should adopt Franklin's core curriculum or keep its own. In the end, Hill made a practical, political decision: he would stay with Middleburg's existing curriculum. In his view, attempting to "switch out" all of his curriculum programs to Franklin's might create significant pockets of resistance in his teaching staff (many of whom liked this or that curriculum program) that could threaten the adoption of the entire plan he was pioneering. (Five years after the arrangement began, when everyone in Middleburg felt much more comfortable, the district actually switched to Franklin's core curriculum—a trend seen in other districts following Middleburg's lead.)

Items 9 and 10 are straightforward enough. Franklin had developed the industry's best "pay for performance" systems, particularly for principals, and Hill wanted to use them. On the financial front, Franklin had always viewed every site as an individual P&L (profit and loss) center, so its budgeting process for sites was highly advanced. (In fact, in those days, many school districts did not even do site-by-site budgets.)

In Item 11, Hill said that he wanted to be able to call upon "at will" certain services within the Franklin system, but only when he needed them. For instance, if he was considering upgrading his technological platform, he would want Franklin's consultation on that. (Middleburg had a technology staff of two at its central office. Franklin, even then, had a technology group of fifty-six—and Hill knew it would grow into the hundreds in the years ahead.)

Finally, in Item 12, Hill believed his would not be the only district to follow this model. He imagined a time when most small and medium-sized districts in the country would be in the type of arrangement he was pioneering. He envisioned that group as an "extended family," learning from one another and together helping to shape the future of what their provider, in this case Franklin, offered to them. He was right beyond his dreams.

Today, Franklin has "affiliate agreements" with 1,300 districts across the United States. These districts meet once a year in a major national conference to see new features unveiled and to discuss their needs with Franklin. Advisory groups meet much more frequently around critical items, and Franklin includes members of the network in all its major R&D arenas. Hill was the first president of the Franklin Affiliate Organization (FAO), and served in that position for over a decade. In some respects, the relationship between Franklin and its affiliate districts is similar to that of major television networks, in which the local stations are owned and operated by local entrepreneurs but have relationships with major national networks for their national programming and news.

Hill's initial presentation of the concept did not deal with what ultimately became an important part of the Middleburg/Franklin discussion: (1) whether the staff would be district employees or Franklin staff members, and (2) who the staff would report to— who would hire, evaluate, and, when necessary, terminate them? On Question 1, the answer turned out to be relatively simple: the staff would be employees of the district and Franklin, thus allowing staff to continue their participation in state retirement systems. Question 2 was more complicated. Franklin had a distinct point of view on this matter. It did not believe it could be effective if it was viewed simply as a "consultant" to the district. While Middleburg's superintendent would clearly be the "boss of Franklin," Franklin needed "partner status" when it came to critical hires, such as principals. Franklin was convinced that without this, it could easily be ignored and would not be able to implement for Middleburg everything that it had learned and developed. Middleburg and Franklin eventually worked out an arrangement to ensure that both parties had a voice in principal selection. The contract stipulated that principals would be hired by Middleburg with significant consultation by Franklin, and that the performance compensation of principals (which was significant) would be jointly discussed each year. In day-to-day operating matters, principals would continue to report directly to Middleburg. The individual selection of teachers was left to principals, though there was a joint district/Franklin committee that ultimately approved all hires.

When Hill presented his idea, he had no idea what it might cost the district. He secretly hoped it would be about 3 percent of his annual budget. That was a number he thought he could find without too much difficulty within the $96 million he spent annually. He asked Franklin to price out his plan. When they did, he was stunned. According to Franklin's estimates, the cost would be closer to 4.5 percent of the district's annual budget, or about $4.5 million per year. At first, Hill thought that was the end of the discussion, having no idea where to find that kind of money. But then the real collaboration between Middleburg and Franklin began. Franklin said to Hill, "Look, what we are charging you is more or less what it costs us *in our own schools*. If Franklin can find this in the budget of its schools, there ought to be a way to find it in Middleburg. Let's look together." And so they did. Hill and a Franklin team studied the amount Middleburg annually spent, looking for ways to fund the collaboration. As Hill had roughly guessed, about 3 percent of that was easy enough to find. Example: The district spent a significant amount on a whole variety of one-off professional-development opportunities (which Franklin and others nicknamed "drive-by training"). These would no longer be necessary. But the final 1.5 percent was more difficult. Ultimately, it had to come from a 2 percent reduction in Middleburg's total staff count. Middleburg's annual attrition rate was about 4 percent, so no one actually lost his or her job, but there were real changes. For example, class size increased by about one student per class. In Hill's view that was a trade-off he could stomach, thinking that the improvement in virtually all his system capabilities would more than offset any academic effect from a one-student change in class size. There were more than a few high-heat school-board meetings during the debate. Dire predictions were made, and Hill needed all his political skill to sell the changes. But he did sell them. And he turned out to be right.

After nine months of debate, discussion, and planning, Middleburg agreed to a ten-year contract with Franklin. Middleburg wanted a five-year arrangement, but Franklin, having learned the importance of adhering to a plan over a substantial period of time, insisted on the longer term. As the affiliate-agreement concept matured in the decades that followed, most contracts became twelve or fifteen years in length.

Middleburg was a solid district when it began with Franklin, with most of its students already proficient on state exams. But within five years Middleburg ranked first in Tennessee, leading the number-two district in the state by three full points. But where Middleburg's results really proved remarkable was in the "below-the-surface" numbers. The second-best district in Tennessee had 19 percent of its children achieving at advanced levels on the state's exams. *Middleburg had double that.* Even more important, Middleburg's children of color had exactly the same percentage of children in the advanced group—*triple* the performance of any other district in the state. In Middleburg, the achievement gap had been completely eliminated.

Dwight Hill plans to retire this year. When he does, Franklin plans to hold a special ceremony at its annual national affiliate meeting to salute the historic role Hill played in U.S. education. Without his vision others might not have followed.

Grawson Schools, 2030

Richard Hamel, the sixty-three-year-old chairman and CEO of Grawson Schools, was sitting pretty and had a pretty view to boot, staring out over the always busy Victoria Harbour from his spacious corner office on Hong Kong Island. In a reflective moment, he was admiring more than the view. Grawson had just won a twenty-year contract to manage 1,000 schools with more than 1 million children in the large Chinese province of Shandong. Though Chinese per-pupil spending on education still lagged behind the West, the contract was worth a great deal to Grawson and firmly established its hold as the schooling leader in Asia. Franklin Schools, the world schooling "co-leader," had secured only 600 schools as part of the competition, making the victory for Hamel and his team even more impressive.

Hamel had moved to Hong Kong in 2018 to head Grawson's global schools company (the division that now dwarfed any other at Grawson) after a highly successful twenty-year run at the New York–based Franklin. It was a daring move. He was among three individuals at Franklin who were likely to succeed Franklin's aging founder. And at the time of his move, it was not at all clear that Grawson would grow into its current position, challenging Franklin for leadership in the global education business. Franklin had a fifteen-year head start.

But Grawson, the worldwide leader in K–12 curricula, had used its financial strength and publishing prowess to catch up. It had also studied all Franklin's early errors and avoided their costs. Just as Airbus and Boeing had duked it out across the globe for supremacy in aviation, so it was now with Grawson and Franklin. In the past decade, Franklin's global enrollment had led in six years, whereas Grawson had won the enrollment crown in four. (Where the Airbus/Boeing analogy fell apart was that the two education leaders had a dozen additional serious competitors to contend with, unlike the aviation giants, who basically split the global market.)

You might be surprised that the schools division of Grawson (a U.S. company) is headquartered in Hong Kong. In 2005, if you had asked even informed players in education whether they thought education would become a global enterprise, almost all would have said no. Yet if you had looked closely, even in those early days of the industry there were already clear signs that the category could well head in a global direction. In 2004, Mosaica, then a charter-school firm out of the United States, was consulting with the Qatar government on the buildup of its educational infrastructure. Sabis, a Beirut-based company that had originally built its reputation running English-speaking schools throughout Europe and the Middle East, was by the late 1990s managing charter schools in the United States. A firm that ran private schools in the United Arab Emirates, GEMS, was moving substantially into Britain in 2004 and was looking to set up shop in the States. And Franklin Schools, the largest U.S. schools player, already had a rapidly growing business in the U.K. by 2005. Even at the turn of the century, these schooling companies seemed to intuit the same thing: education should be a global service. The languages people spoke were different, but the process through which children learned was universal, techniques of instruction traveled well, and significant portions of curriculum (the most notable examples being math and science) were effectively "global languages" already. These companies seemed to get one other thing: if education was to stay relevant and strong, it was important that it lead, not lag, larger societal trends. Though a McDonald's arch in Shanghai offended the aesthetic sensibilities of many, the trend toward a global village was irreversible. Even the French had come to accept that Disney was not a dragon to be feared.

Grawson was the first of the world's major communications and publishing companies to grasp fully that the world of schooling was an extension of the core competencies found in many communications entities. Despite the immense operational aspects of schooling that had to be mastered, Grawson's management understood that leadership in the education industry would be differentiated by superior school design, great information and assessment skills, terrific recruitment and training capability, and highly creative, online curriculum. Grawson had either leads or "base camps" in most of these in 2000. They had flirted with jumping into the category in the 1990s as they watched Franklin's dramatic launch and its clear ability to move schools forward academically. They hesitated for two big reasons. First, Franklin had taken a brutal whipping in the press in its early days. Union and union-backed opponents, initially believing that Franklin was a right-wing plot to bust unions and even public education itself, had succeeded in distorting the company's true academic contribution and had painted it as profit-mongering capitalism at its worst. Second, if Franklin's academic bottom line had been impressive, its financial one had not. It took Franklin over a decade and nearly a billion dollars to find its way to profitability.

Two events moved Grawson to act. First, between 2004 and 2006, Franklin's financial position improved dramatically. It exited some early relationships that were depressing its bottom line and focused on replicating the kinds of client arrangements that had worked well academically and financially, like its great early successes on the East Coast. Second, two legislative events convinced Grawson that the world of schooling was about to take off. In 2004 the Blair government unveiled its Building Schools of the Future (BSF) initiative, which would ultimately involve the private sector in thousands of British schools. Then, as part of the NCLB reauthorization in 2007, the bipartisan Alexander–Kennedy Education Innovation Act was passed, dramatically ramping up research and development spending in K–12 education. The act funded the creation and launch of three major new school designs and their related support systems in the United States. Grawson bet that the K–12 schooling industry, long viewed as the "steepest face" of the world education mountain, was about to enter an era of hypergrowth. The company jumped into the fray in both Britain and the United States, winning, along with Franklin and Schools for Children, one of the three R&D contracts under the Alexander–Kennedy Act to develop and launch new designs in the States.

What Grawson had achieved since it decided to compete was stunning.

As it was in 2005, education remains the second-largest industry in many developed countries, second only to health care, with more than 1.5 billion school-aged children in the world. Economists predict, however, that education will overtake health care worldwide in spending by 2060. The 2015 Nobel Prize–winning work of Laurie Le, which proved that higher spending in education actually leads to physically healthier societies (and, therefore, lower health care costs), is affecting government spending priorities across the globe. What is hugely different from 2005 is the role of private providers in education. What happened is similar to what happened in health care in the United States in the last three decades of the last century. In 1969 health care companies represented only 2 percent of the market capitalization of all U.S. public companies. By 2000, that number had risen tenfold, to 23 percent. Similarly, in 2005 national and global education providers enrolled less than 1 percent of children on the globe. Today, they represent only 4 percent of the world's school-age children, but consider what that means: they are educating just over 60 million students, and their combined revenues are approximately $300 billion. Grawson and Franklin are the two largest, with approximately a 10 percent share of market, enrollments of roughly 6 million each, and annual revenues of $25 and $28 billion, respectively. In *Fortune*'s list of the world's one thousand largest companies, they are now ranked 160th and 165th. Equally important, nine other schooling companies are now in *Fortune*'s "World's Top 1,000 Companies."

Of course, it was not always so. In 2005, Grawson had no revenue in this category, and Franklin was only a $500 million entity. By 2010, Franklin was a bit over $1 billion in size, and Grawson was gaining rapidly. Against "big-company" standards, both were still relative peanuts. But each has subsequently grown at roughly a 20 percent compounded rate for two decades. Though that may sound remarkable—to sustain a 20 percent compounded growth rate off a $1 billion base for twenty years—Grawson was not even close to the first company to do it. In 1980, Wal-Mart was a $1 billion entity. Twenty-five years later, it was $256 billion, the world's largest company, and it achieved that by a compounded annual growth rate of 25 percent for *twenty-five years*. (In 2005 alone, it increased its annual sales by $25 billion.) From 1984 to 2005, Dell grew from $0 to $49 billion. And to do that, Dell had to capture 19 percent of the personal computer market, over double the share Grawson needed to achieve its position.

As Hamel relished his beautiful view, he thought back to the old days and marveled at the difference in schools of the world today. He had presented a chart recently, in a worldwide videoconference for all Grawson managers, dramatically illustrating the point:

	2000–2030: THE BENEFITS OF SCALE	
	AVERAGE U.S. SCHOOL DISTRICT IN 2000	GRAWSON SCHOOLS IN 2030
Enrollment served	3,300	6 million
Number of schools served	6	12,000
Revenues	$28 million	$25 billion
Percentage of amount spent at school site	75%	80%
Percentage of amount spent on school support systems	25%	7%
Percentage of amount spent on R&D	0%	3%
Pretax profit	0%	10%
Actual amount spent on support systems annually	$7 million	$1.75 billion
Actual amount spent on R&D annually	0	$750 million

Though Hamel enjoyed leading a $25 billion entity, scale itself had never been his objective. *What he cared about was what could be done with scale, how scale could affect the quality of a school.* He recalled the early days of the schooling industry, when the politically correct view was "Smaller is better" and when he was often attacked by an association called Small Matters. Small classes, small schools, and small systems—all of these were in vogue. Whether there was much (or any) research to support any of this did not seem to matter greatly. The idea simply resonated with the public at the time. If you were to ask a woman on the street, "Quick, which do you want for your child: a class of twelve or a class of thirty?" the answer would, of course, be twelve. Pollsters did not put the question in a more nuanced way, like: "Less quickly, which do you want for your child: a class of twelve with an unqualified teacher and no technological support *or* a class of thirty with a highly qualified, well-trained teacher and marvelous technological systems?" What Hamel knew then, and later helped the broader public to understand, was this: Cottage-industry mentality might be cute and cozy, it might appeal to our desire to return to a certain quaint innocence, but it cannot confront the immensely complex challenges of educating more than 1.5 billion children around the globe.

And so what Hamel most enjoyed about the chart were two statistics: (1) the absolute dollars spent in support systems at Grawson today versus what an average school system in 2000 had spent ($1.75 billion versus $7 million); and (2) the difference between what used to be spent in school R&D and what was now being spent. In the year 2000, R&D spending on schools was effectively $0, not even a line item in most school-system budgets. (There was some R going on at universities, but there was almost no D going on anywhere.) An average school system's scale was so small that a typical district simply could not afford to develop state-of-the-art systems. In his recent videoconference presentation to global managers at Grawson, Hamel highlighted four key differences between typical district systems of the past and Grawson's capabilities today—all of which had been brought about by the advantages of scale.

(Let's take a quick look at each, but before we do, let me note that these types of capabilities, or analogues of such, existed within virtually all large companies *in 2005, twenty-five years ago! Their analogues just did not exist in U.S. school systems, primarily because of a lack of scale.*)

PLU

In 2015 Grawson opened its Principal Leadership University (PLU), in Palo Alto, California, in partnership with the Schools of Business and Education at Stanford. Each year, Grawson Schools needs approximately 1,800 new principals—900 to launch the new schools it is opening and 900 replacement principals for its existing 12,000 schools. Grawson learned early on that site leadership was a crucial ingredient in success. Between its launch in 2005 and 2015, it had been building its leadership-development capabilities. PLU at Palo Alto, now a globally recognized institution in the world of education, was a huge step for Grawson—and one that clearly illustrated the value of scale. In the year 2000, the average school district in the United States had six principals, making it impossible for that district to build up any true expertise in principal training and development. That task was left to hundreds of schools of education at colleges and universities that might, in a given year, have a few dozen potential principal candidates going through rather "generic and general" courses that might or might not relate to the schools in which they would later work.

To become a "Grawson principal," a candidate must complete a rigorous four-year course of study: two years in Palo Alto and the other two as an "intern principal" at a Grawson site, very similar to a medical student's training program. Only 25 percent of those applying to PLU are accepted. Just to apply one must meet three qualifications: (1) a bachelor's degree, (2) at least three years of teaching, and (3) a 1350 on the PR-SAT (a special and proprietary variation of the SAT that Grawson asked the Educational Testing Service to develop). PLU is not like an Ivy League school, at which acceptance virtually guarantees graduation. Of those who begin the course of study, 30 percent are "washed out," which means that only 1 in 6 *who are qualified* ultimately make it. Through special arrangements with Stanford, candidates receive a joint master's in education/MBA, but graduation from PLU is worth more than those degrees. Everyone in education (and beyond) knows that being a Grawson principal is a highly prestigious post, that you have graduated from the equivalent of the West Point of education. And the economics are nothing to sneeze at either. In 2005 dollars, a Grawson principal can make about $250,000, with a base of $150,000 and up to $100,000 based on his or her school's student achievement scores and financial results—and that is *before* the stock plan. Finally, graduating from PLU is one of the best ways to rise through the ranks of Grawson Schools, though not the only way. Seventy percent of Grawson's middle and senior managers have been principals at its schools.

Most important, principals come out remarkably trained to manage a school. Grawson's principals are required to be both achievement experts and excellent business managers, and their course work (modeled largely on the case study method originally developed at Harvard Business School) is divided equally between the two disciplines. One of Hamel's favorite case studies is the "We're Good Enough" case. It presents principal candidates with a school in which 97 percent of students are achieving at proficient or advanced levels. A certain smugness has set in among faculty, parents, and students. The challenge was how to get the school to think beyond the limits of the conventional assessment system. One team of principals (groups of four work on cases) developed a solution that is now famous within the lore of Grawson. They created a plan to get teachers and students at the "case school" to prove how the current assessment system did not go deep enough in its analysis of student capabilities. In other words, they designed a test that spurred improved achievement by broadening and deepening the standards used in the assessment engine. (Their work actually led to an upgrade in Grawson's assessment engine.)

All this is not cheap. Of the $1.75 billion that Grawson spends on "school support systems," PLU consumes about $300 million. The great bulk of that is the cost of the 3,600 principal candidates who are on site in Palo Alto in any given year. Grawson picks up a portion of that tab, and then lends candidates the balance. The cost also includes the PLU faculty, another 150 individuals, who for the most part were previously "top-gun" Grawson principals, and operation of the center (which also runs the continuing-education program for active principals). PLU hosts its own "leadership research-and-development institute," but that $50 million is budgeted through Grawson's R&D function, not through PLU itself. Grawson's total tab on initial principal education, continuing principal education, and leadership R&D is $350 million per year, over ten times the total operating budget of a typical U.S. school district. It is a lot of money, but Hamel views it as a crucial part of Grawson's competitive advantage—and just one example of what scale can accomplish.

Grawson's investment in principal development is actually dwarfed by its spending on teacher professional development. The Grawson Teaching Institute, housed in the same building with Hamel in Hong Kong, provides international conferences and professional development to Grawson's 300,000 teachers with an annual budget just north of $500 million. Unlike PLU, which has a small-enough group of principal candidates to be housed at one site, most teacher professional development is done through videoconference and online instruction. There is one exception: initial, intense 90-day teacher "boot camps" at various sites around the globe. But that's another story.

SIC

Six thousand miles east of Palo Alto, in Cambridge, England, is the second unit that Hamel highlighted in his recent company presentation. Known around the company simply as SIC, it is every bit as important to Grawson Schools as SAC (the Strategic Air Command) was to the United States during the Cold War. SIC is short for the Student Information Center. The name is a bit out of date, as it is now both the Staff and Student Information Center. SIC stores and protects electronic information on everyone the company serves and employs. A 500-person, $200 million-per-year facility and unit run in partnership with IBM, it is the worldwide data hub of the company. As one enters the building, a motto in the lobby—"Accurate, Anytime, Anyplace"—illustrates SIC's commitment to provide the entire global organization with high-quality, real-time information.

In the late twentieth century, the first electronic student-information systems were introduced. These kept basic information about students like attendance and home addresses. During that same time, serious student assessment was an every-once-in-a-while affair, sometimes every three or four years, such as at the third-, fifth-, and eighth-grade levels. It wasn't really viewed as part of the instructional mechanism. It was a relatively primitive way to assess how school systems were performing, and one that was sometimes polluted by political interests. Often there was a punitive or even "let's embarrass everyone" mode to it, with some states making a spectacle of the annual publication of the data, often gleefully highlighting failure. And there was nothing "real-time" about it. Schools often waited six months to get data back, long after students had left the class—or even the school—in which they had been tested.

Between 2000 and 2010, there was a movement toward making assessment part of the day-to-day work of teachers. It was as if policy makers had discovered something the medical community had learned a century earlier: that diagnosis was the first step in treatment. Various companies came up with systems to electronically monitor the progress of children on a quarterly or monthly basis and report this in real time to teachers. The objective was to help teachers formulate instructional strategies for each child through frequent assessment. Many credit the introduction of these systems with the general rise in student performance during that decade. Before entering the school management field, Grawson had been a provider of one of these systems (as well as a student-information system). It built on this expertise to create SIC, mainly between 2010 and 2020. As curriculum increasingly went online between 2005 and 2020, SIC became the repository of Grawson's electronic curriculum systems as well. (SIC, though, was not a "creator" of curriculum. That was housed elsewhere in Grawson Schools—at 3C, soon to be discussed.)

SIC is a marvel, and a tool any Grawson principal or teacher would simply be lost without. Members of the Grawson family— which includes principals, teachers, students, and parents—have varying degrees of access to the databank, with the proper authorization codes, from any location worldwide. In seconds, an authorized teacher can pull up the entire academic history of his or her students to see strengths and weaknesses in various subject strands, identify good or troubling trends in performance, or monitor (and aid) a student's progress on all of his or her curriculum assignments. Similarly, a student can see virtually all the same reports. (Part of the Grawson culture is a student's responsibility for his or her own learning path. As the mantra goes around Grawson, "It's your life. Better learn it.")

One part of the system Hamel finds most impressive is the "critical care index." SIC is automatically programmed to track and "merge" multiple factors in a student's performance, including the electronic filing of homework, weekly assessments of progress, attendance, illness, discipline incidents, even a student's self-assessment of his or her attitude. The system is able to combine these into an overall index. Should that index reach a particular threshold level, SIC alerts, simultaneously, the teacher, student, principal, and parents, and provides each with research-based suggestions and protocols. Everyone at Grawson knows that SIC is not a substitute for teacher, parent, or student judgments, skills, and intuition. It is simply a tool, but a tool every bit as valuable as all those screens in the cockpit of a modern-day jetliner.

(SIC does not contain the Grawson Library. That was outsourced in 2015 to Google when it became clear that Google would emerge as the preeminent creator of custom, global, online libraries.)

3C

3C is Grawson's shorthand for the Curriculum Creation Center. Similar to the way cable companies had merged or become connected in some way to movie studios in the 1980s and 1990s (think distribution merging with content), Grawson Schools had taken over the old "textbook" part of Grawson in 2017. In the early days of schooling companies, curriculum had been purchased "off the shelf" from publishers. As the industry emerged,

Grawson Schools and competitors found themselves often adapting curriculum to the idiosyncrasies of their own school designs. Further, they often had to do the same kind of "workaround" in their professional-development/training programs. Most major schooling companies decided to integrate vertically by creating their own curriculum capabilities, either building them from scratch or acquiring existing publishers.

Wanting a significant HQ presence on all continents, Grawson had decided to split 3C into two major facilities, one housed on the coast near Rio de Janeiro (in what was now referred to as Silicon Beach around the company) and the other in Cape Town. Hamel loved to visit the Cape Town facility, which housed 2,000 of Grawson's most creative staff members. 3C was divided into fourteen different curriculum "labs," such as reading, math, science, languages, music, and art. Cape Town had seven of those fourteen labs. Each created the lessons and projects constituting courses of studies for each subject area. In addition, they designed the assessments and teacher professional-development programs for their subject areas. (One of the fourteen labs was the "interdisciplinary" unit, which created the yearlong senior projects that every Grawson student had to complete for graduation.) Everything was done digitally, and printing was rare, although print capabilities were available at every school site for those few students who still preferred print to their electronic tablets.

Grawson is known for its excellence in the "core fields" of reading, science, and math. Grawson won the recent China contract in part because of the Chinese government's concern that its students were increasingly falling behind those in America and Europe—and particularly those in Grawson Schools. But when Hamel visits Cape Town, he always stops by two "offbeat" labs. One is formally called the Motivation Lab and informally known as the Arsonists, an adaptation of what was originally the Fire-starters. Its charge is to study ways to increase student motivation, and most important, it provides Grawson's schools with a variety of motivational programs. The one schools find indispensable is the Daily Interview. In this unit, Grawson researchers discovered that the single most effective student-motivation factor was what they called "identification with excellence." Meeting a number of people who did something, anything, extremely well increased students' motivation to learn. What the people they met actually did seemed to matter little. The fact that they did it well is what made the difference. Equally important, the researchers observed a "cluster effect"—that is, even if students did not wish to pursue the career or specialty they were hearing about, they began to "abstract" the concept of excellence through multiple exposures to successful people. To deliver this phenomenon, Grawson created a remarkably inexpensive worldwide system of "student interview teams." After extensive research, a student team is dispatched to interview a political leader, musician, scientist, athlete, or religious leader who personifies excellence. The interview is edited by the lab into a succinct fifteen-minute piece that airs on Grawson's global School Network every day. Grawson can gain access to virtually anyone for these interviews for two reasons. First, who doesn't like to be presented as a model of excellence to the world's children? And second, many leaders have a message that they certainly do not mind delivering to 6 million students. (Grawson's television unit had actually asked to sell advertising on the interviews, but remembering all the controversy that Channel One, an early pioneer in school TV, had endured, Hamel said, "Who needs all that trouble for only $80 million in ad revenues?" Another advantage of scale.)

Then there is the lab called Well-Being, the staff members of which are called wellbees around Grawson. Initially set up as

Grawson's physical fitness lab, this group has been credited with substantially decreasing childhood obesity among Grawson students. In its first decade of existence, it focused mainly on physical health, but at Hamel's urging, its portfolio of responsibilities has increased over the last decade to include elements of mental and emotional health. The high school curriculum of all Grawson students now includes a form of group discussions as well as a new strain of "self-analysis." A series of questions in Grawson's assessment battery related to well-being tracks how students feel about themselves. It is part of the "critical care index" earlier referenced.

The DC

The concept of "whole-school design" first became popular in the 1990s. As we look back, this concept seems rather obvious, but at the time few people had thought about approaching schools in their totality. People trying to change schools tended to simply work on one element, like math or student discipline, but not on the entire design itself. Franklin Schools was one of the first to bring this concept to life, and later many other entities adopted the approach.

Of course as schooling companies emerged, this became a critical part of their intellectual property. In business language, some call it the "store model." Each major school company now has school designs that are either patented or trademarked, and each, in varying degrees, has important R&D units working on future designs, no different from the way auto companies or drug companies have significant research facilities looking for their next breakthroughs.

At Grawson, this unit is called the DC, short for the School Design Center, on a campus in Princeton, New Jersey. To understand it, think of the test track of an auto company or the wind tunnel of an aeronautics firm. Grawson does not like the idea of trying out new school designs during the regular school year (which potentially distracts from children's education), so it decided to test its new school designs during optional summer programs. In a recent visit to Princeton several summers ago, Hamel had seen some new school-design tests in the works. Two were particularly radical.

One is derisively called Lord of the Flies by those around the company who believe it is far-fetched. It is a high school design in which virtually *everything* at a school is run by the students. There are only five adults on the campus; they serve as the "board" of the school and "monitor" student behavior, but they have no operating roles in the school. (Hamel actually thinks it has some promise and recently increased its R&D budget to go into second-stage trials.) Another design is called the Glass Bead Game, named after the Hermann Hesse novel of the 1940s. The idea is that, beginning in middle school, the entire curriculum is a seven-year puzzle. To solve the puzzle, students have to learn everything that would normally be learned in an advanced Grawson curriculum. (Hamel views this one as less promising and has allowed one more year to show some results.)

If a school design (or elements of a design) shows significant promise, Grawson launches it in a region or country for a couple of years before determining whether to roll it out to customers globally. Currently Grawson offers its clients (school districts, states, and nations) four different designs. Three others are in various stages of advanced testing.

Back to Hamel in Hong Kong. 3C, SIC, the DC, and PLU are what make his role particularly interesting. They also make schools and school systems hugely different from, and so much more successful than, what they were twenty-five years ago. When he started his career with Franklin in 2000, no system, including Franklin, had the scale to develop such capacities. Now they are commonplace—compelling examples of the great things that scale brings to schools—no different from those in other sectors.

Hamel stopped his reflective moment, got up from his desk, and headed to an afternoon meeting. He had heard that New York City was firing a smaller competitor of Grawson's. He wanted to know why, wanted to make sure Grawson's head was not on the block as well, and wanted the schools the competitor was losing. Just another day at the office.

PART IV

Laws and Leadership

CHAPTER 9

Homeland Offense— The Next Wave of Reform Legislation

I f you look back across the history of America, you can see that a number of legislative and executive acts have changed the face of our country and the world. NASA, Social Security, the Civil Rights Act, the Manhattan Project, the Interstate Highway Act, and the century-spanning buildup of the National Institutes of Health are a few good examples. All were brought to us by visionary political leaders. All were actions that because of their scale or sweeping importance could not be initiated by cities or states. And many were brought about by unique, long, and complex partnerships with the private sector.

This chapter is one observer's notion of the blueprint of an act that could have similar far-reaching effects on K–12 schooling in the United States. Lawmaker I am not. So it is my hope that two representatives or two senators, one Democrat and one Republican, will embrace the thinking here, make it better, and turn it into a sweeping new education bill, the Education Innovation Act of 2007, an act that, soon and one hundred years from now, will be viewed as having set a new course for U.S. schooling. Perhaps it could become a "second act" of NCLB. Most of it attempts to help districts and schools that NCLB will highlight as requiring assistance. As its title suggests, the bill is not about coercion, regulation, rules, or punishment. It is not the bungling, intrusive hand of big government run amok. Nor is it the abdication of public education to the private sector. It is fundamentally about seeking, nurturing, and inspiring breakthroughs. It is designed to help American K–12 education deal with its difficult, thorny, and persistent problems in ways never before seen.

But first, to introduce this, let me provide some recent historical context.

During the past fifteen years, state and federal legislation has played a crucial role in the school-reform/school-improvement movement. Legislators paved the way for the most important innovations now being played out in America's schools. Without legislative action, we would not have seen the progress that has been made. Without legislative action, there would not be the constellation of entities that now makes up the school-reform/school-improvement community—entities with the capacity to be deployed by the government as a launching pad for things much greater.

In the two decades ahead, lawmakers will have an even more pivotal role. First, they must defend and improve laws already in place; the counterattack to undo, diminish, and water down these measures is well under way. If not properly countered, these reactionary moves will be damaging, perhaps mortally, to the cause of building schools of excellence. Second, and of perhaps greater importance, America needs a second wave of landmark legislation to complete the job intended by laws enacted in the past twenty years.

Three key types of legislation have affected schools since the late 1980s: state-by-state charter-school acts (the primary manifestation of the "choice movement"); state takeover laws, such as Pennsylvania's innovative reform of the school district of Philadelphia; and the federal No Child Left Behind Act, supported by various related state regulations (the key success of the "accountability movement").

As noted earlier, the charter-school laws passed by forty states and the District of Columbia have made possible the creation of 3,300 new schools, which now educate nearly 800,000 students, approaching 2 percent of U.S. schoolchildren. In the view of parents, the great majority of these students were not being well served by their prior schools. These families chose a new option. And they believe their children are now better off. As this movement is very young, large-scale objective studies of its results have yet to appear. There is, however, plenty of evidence beyond people "voting with their feet"—evidence from early studies and from substantial numbers of specific situations—that these charter public schools are performing for students and placing friendly competitive pressure on traditional public schools. I would argue, however, that the fact that these laws aided the creation of several significant "alternative-education providers" of both for-profit and nonprofit classes is of even greater importance. We have only begun to see the impact of these new entities.

Opponents of the charter-school movement are hard at work to stem the growth of charters. Their tactics include sponsorship and dissemination of biased and faulty achievement information, moves to cap how many charters can be created, and efforts to prohibit or diminish the most effective and larger charter entities from further scaling their operations—for example, by allowing them only "one campus" or prohibiting the use of professional school managers, especially for-profit ones, altogether. Legislators need to vigorously defend these charter laws, which have brought more reform to America's schools than any other single legislation in the past two decades. By defending such legislation, lawmakers will also defend the entities that will move school reform to greater heights in the years ahead, a fact very well understood by the enemies of school reform.

State takeovers of troubled (usually large, urban) districts have a spotty record. Too often, they have amounted to nothing more than a change in the nameplate on the door. One laudable exception was Pennsylvania's 2001 takeover of the school district of Philadelphia, as implemented by the School Reform Commission that the law created and by Paul Vallas, the CEO it hired.

That law, as implemented by the commission, has spawned a promising model that one can see in my sketches of public education of the future. The multiprovider model was created and first tested in Philadelphia, and the results are beyond encouraging. Philadelphia has gone from a district with average annual gains of less than 1 percentage point to one with average annual gains of more than 7 percentage points. The human benefits behind those numbers are staggering. Edison's twenty schools in Philadelphia, some of the toughest in the district, went up by an extraordinary 10.5 percentage points in the 2003–2004 school year alone. The multiprovider model in Philadelphia includes a wide range of partners, including for-profit companies such as Edison, all operating under a productive competition created by a reform-minded public management team. It is a model for the nation.

In addition to charter laws and state takeover legislation, the federal NCLB act of 2002 instituted the toughest accountability standards in the nation's history. Under NCLB, all schools are required to achieve adequate yearly progress (AYP), and if they fail to do so, a number of sanctions can be put in place, including new governance and new management of these schools. The impact of this law on student achievement in America has already been significant. Here's an example: In order to compare and contrast the performance of its own schools, Edison has monitored a group of over 1,000 underperforming schools across the United States. For years, annual achievement gains in these schools were slightly over 1 point. Suddenly, following the passage of NCLB, average gains in these schools increased to nearly triple historic levels. We believe NCLB is the primary stimulus, as we cannot identify any other variable that would have affected such a large control sample.

Given the complexity of NCLB, legitimate refinements are being put forth by many. These should be considered. But there is also a movement afoot to extract the teeth of this legislation. Federal lawmakers, and state legislators and regulators, need to carefully assess what is a refinement and what is self-interested emasculation masquerading as refinement. Steadfast support of this law is important in keeping schools focused on results—and in providing consequences in the event results do not materialize for children. Put another way: As consequences are called for, the federal government must not blink. Additionally, continuing strength in this legislation will accelerate the growth of alternative-education providers—who, because of the advantages of scale, are primary engines of improvement—as school districts focus more and more on finding new ways to achieve NCLB's mandated results.

So what should lawmakers be considering to propel a "second wave" that takes American education to another level? If, broadly speaking, legislation of the past two decades was about (1) creating an environment for choice and competition and (2) raising the bar for achievement, then legislation of the near future should have two new, related themes: (1) the creation of more "supply" and (2) supporting much greater innovation. It is one thing to have the *ability* to choose a school; it's another thing entirely to actually *have* better schools to choose from. Legislators have worked hard to bring a degree of "free markets" to American schools. In addition to defending and expanding those free markets, their focus should be expanded to enhance the likelihood that there is *ample and quality supply within those markets.* America's parents need and deserve many more new schools from which to choose, and those schools must be materially better and different. If the past fifteen years have been about breaking down barriers to entry, the next fifteen should be about nurturing and propelling innovation on a scale not previously known in American education. The fields have been plowed. It is time to plant on a much wider basis.

Before proposing what this new legislation might seek to create, it is important to give the reader some context from which to judge its scale, its practicality, and its methods. Enter two analogues: (1) the relationship between the Department of Defense and defense contractors and (2) the relationship between the National Institutes of Health and America's medical research community.

America has the finest and most modern military on the face of the earth. Our military is so advanced in conventional capacity that no other country on the globe can possibly compete. The results of both the Desert Storm and Iraqi Freedom campaigns clearly demonstrate this fact. Both saw a substantial military force, the Iraqis, completely and quickly overwhelmed by the U.S. military without the mention, much less the use, of our nuclear arsenals.

If you think the American military is so good because of how much we spend, think again. The combined budgets of the Army, Navy, Marines, and Air Force and all other aspects of the Department of Defense *are roughly equal to what we spend on public education in America.* If spending alone were the road to excellence, it would be logical to assume that our schools would be better than they are. The American military is successful for many reasons, spending being only one of them. Another factor has played an equally important role: the Department of Defense's partnerships with the private sector. DoD looks to its private partners as a major source of innovation, and it purposefully deploys and spurs them to that end. Our ships, planes, tanks, intelligence equipment, missiles, satellites, certain training programs, and on and on—virtually all were created by an intense and deep public/private interaction that dates back two centuries.

Let's consider an example. In the late 1980s, DoD determined that it needed a replacement for the F-15 fighter, the primary "strike fighter" used by our armed services (as well as many of our allies around the globe). DoD laid out its desired "reforms"—a set of specifications for this new generation of fighter, the F-22 (speed, payload, etc.). In 1991, it provided $9.5 billion in development dollars to Boeing and Lockheed Martin, asking them to design and build the first nine planes. Let me put this $9.5 billion in some perspective: it is almost 40 times what the federal government spends in education R&D on an annual basis. Yes, the design of just one weapon's platform received 40 times our nation's annual support of educational design! When the DoD determines something is important to the nation's security, it *ensures* that the private sector pulls out all the stops to create possible alternatives. The government provides the seed capital, often sums unapproachable even to the largest private-sector institutions, to create such options. Then it chooses the best to produce. (Ultimately, Boeing won the competition, and it is estimated that DoD will pay Boeing an additional $60 *billion* dollars to build 330 of these aircraft.)

Now ask yourself two questions. First, is the performance of our schools important to national security and the state of our union? Unequivocally, yes. Second, has anything approaching what was just described ever happened in the field of education? For instance, has the Department of Education ever put out a "request for proposals" funded by even hundreds of millions asking major companies or organizations to provide America not with a design for our next "strike fighter" but with higher-performing designs for our elementary schools, middle schools, and high schools for the next thirty years? Has the federal government ever put out a similar request for new designs for teacher colleges or principal colleges, the entities that provide absolutely critical ingredients to the success of our schools? Unequivocally, no.

In the early 1990s, the first Bush administration, under the leadership of Lamar Alexander as secretary of education, took a visionary step in this direction, albeit on a tiny scale. The feds jump-started a small private-sector entity called New American Schools. Federal dollars were not even involved. Instead, the administration used its bully pulpit to ask the business community and philanthropists to pitch in. The objective of New American Schools was to provide seed capital to entities exploring new school designs. Grants, again not from public coffers, were tiny by military standards, averaging $1 million to $3 million for new thoughts on school designs. They were provided to a number of private-sector entities. Though some new ideas came from this, they were understandably limited, given the scale of the effort. In comparison with the DoD example, it was the equivalent of the funding for the pilot's seat cushion in the F-22.

The largest "new school design" attempted in the United States was that of Edison Schools, when it raised $45 million to work on its school design. At the time, many viewed this as a gargantuan sum. In comparison with what we see at DoD, it was not even walking-around money. (School design, as noted in Chapter 2, does not mean "architectural design." It means the design of *every* aspect of a school, from curriculum to schedule to organization to budget.)

Under the current Bush administration, there have been some additional promising steps. In 2002, President Bush signed into law the Education Sciences Reform Act of 2002, establishing a new organization, the Institute of Education Sciences. (The old Office of Educational Research and Improvement, which had formerly been responsible for education research and statistics, became part of this new entity.) The new Institute of Education Sciences reflects the administration's intent to provide more resources to the field of education research. But the institute includes more than R&D functions. Large portions of its budget go to tracking the nation's educational results. If you unpack the "pure" R&D number, it is $260 million, a number that pales in comparison to spending on R&D in defense.

The Department of Defense is not the only place where the federal government and the private sector interact in a major way to bring about critical innovations for our country's well-being. Federally coordinated health care R&D is truly institutionalized in the United States. The National Institutes of Health traces its roots back to 1887 and has a record of congressional appropriations dating back to 1938. Today, the NIH invests over $27 billion of federal money *each year* in grants for research on breakthrough medical solutions, *approximately 100 times the federal investment in educational research.* Does that perhaps give us some understanding of why we have the best health care on the globe? Similarly, might it provide a clue as to why our schools are struggling? Is there, perhaps, a lesson here for education policy makers?

When the NIH spots an ominous health threat or when it sees an important opportunity to advance the nation's health, it places significant national resources to work ensuring that these issues are addressed. And like DoD, it does that largely through a long and successful collaboration with the private sector. To give you a sense of its scale relative to the new Institute of Education Sciences, the NIH has over twenty-seven different "centers" of research, each tasked with a particular area of research, and *each one* is, on average, approximately four times as large as the entire federal educational research budget. In the United States, we spend over $1.5 trillion per year on health care, and against this, the federal government is investing $27 billion per year in R&D to *make it better.* The United States spends roughly $400 billion a year on K–12 education. If we were to spend an equivalent percentage on educational R&D to what we spend on health R&D, our educational research expenditures would be approximately $8 billion, or *30 times current expenditure levels.*

Clearly the situation begs this question: Why aren't we investing proportionately? Why don't we have the equivalent of the NIH in the education sector? Twenty years ago, *A Nation at Risk* literally put the threat to our nation's future of school failure in America on the same level as invasion from abroad. If we truly believe that—and we must—why have we not seen more serious support of innovation by the federal government?

I attribute our failure to fund "serious educational innovation investment" to four factors: (1) a federal inattentiveness, grounded in a long-standing bias toward local control of our schools, (2) a failure of our collective imagination about what we might actually discover by significantly funding better school research and development, (3) a lack of seriousness about education in the United States, and (4) our lack of true appreciation—beyond lip service—that superior public K–12 education is perhaps the *only* way America can maintain its leadership on the world stage in the centuries ahead. Let's look at each.

The federal government has been a reluctant participant in K–12, letting schooling, like fire and police protection, remain largely an activity of states and local entities. Until recently, the feds limited their role largely to supplying additional funding for underprivileged children. From time to time, they have also applied pressure for better performance via various bully-pulpit techniques. The NCLB act and federal support of charter-school funding represent new levels of federal involvement, but again, these were designed to open markets and prod performance by shining a light on both failure and success. As for *how* greater numbers of options were to come about and *what* those options might be, the feds left that to the marketplace and school districts to determine. The problem with this strategy is twofold. First, school districts do not have the resources (and in some cases the inclination) to come up with serious new options. The average school district in the United States has a budget of only $28 million. Asking such a district to come up with a serious new school design is similar to asking the police force of Peoria to design an aircraft carrier. It's not going to happen. Second, the K–12 private sector is not yet sufficiently developed to do what needs to be done without federal support. Some might inquire why the private sector doesn't put up the cash. First, the private sector *has* done a great deal. Edison alone has raised around $700 million to support the creation and build-out of its schools, but much of that has gone into real estate and the funding of operational losses in its early years. Over time, the private sector can do more and more of the R&D spending (just as happens in health care), but to ask a fledgling industry to shoulder *all* the burden would be the equivalent of delaying the introduction of the Salk vaccine until the private sector mustered support to fund it. Further to this point, the health care industry, primarily pharmaceuticals, dwarfs the private-sector players in education, and yet the federal government continues to invest side by side with that industry's substantial sums in health care R&D.

Perhaps equally to blame for our inaction is the prevailing view that "all that can be discovered has been discovered" in school design. You might think I'm kidding here or intentionally over-stating the point. I'm not. Very significant numbers within the education community would say the following, either openly or implicitly: "We don't need to worry about new designs in educa-tion. *Everyone already knows what we need to do in schools.* What we have is a failure to execute. If we just had more money to do what we already know, everything would be fine." I cannot tell you how many times I've heard this sentiment. It's like an aircraft designer in the 1930s saying, "We know how to make an airplane go. It's called a propeller. To go faster, we've just got to figure out how to make it spin at a greater rate." Having been immersed in our pub-lic schools now for fifteen years, I can tell you this *is* the prevail-ing view. It leads to the following: "Why conduct serious R&D if we already know what to do?" And this we-already-know-what-to-do view is intuitively supported by laymen as well. Most of us spent twelve to twenty years in traditionally designed schools. It is hard for us to imagine there might be a better way.

Third, if you assume that behavior is the most obvious indica-tor of belief, then our paltry spending on educational research and development is a good indicator of how much we actually value education as a society. Though every politician and editorial writer in America talks the talk on the importance of our schools, our actions say this rhetoric is more political correctness than heartfelt belief. (How could it be otherwise when we systematically send wholly inexperienced teachers into our most needy classrooms?) On some fundamental level, it appears, we really don't believe in the value of schooling. Perhaps all the boring and never-used information we have long since forgotten eroded our national belief in the importance of our schools.

Finally, as a country, we might not yet see the importance of schools in our continued world leadership. After all, though our school performance has been flat for decades according to the NAEP, America's economic position in the world has been secure enough. Yet many believe that security will come to an end in this century. China's middle-class population will soon approach America's *entire* population. And then there is India. America's scale, once one of the key factors in our dominance, will no longer be one of our competitive advantages. Similarly, while America's Calvinist "work ethic" may create higher productivity than that of some European countries, we are unlikely to out-work the Chinese. To remain a player on the world stage, we must outthink, outimagine, and outinnovate our competitors. We must become or remain, in as many sectors as possible, the creative capital of the world. How will we enhance our thinking and our creativity? Can there be any other answer than through our schools? While our focus for the past two decades has been to deal with the deficiency of our schools, our focus in the future must be that *plus* the introduction of a new level of excellence.

So now is the time for federal leadership. It is leadership that is appropriate, it is leadership that will be welcomed, and it is leadership that is timely.

It is appropriate because the federal government explicitly exists to do what cannot be done by our cities and states. Just as our states cannot field a global military, fund large-scale medical breakthroughs, or launch Mars missions, they also cannot tackle the complex and costly efforts to bring systematic new school designs and new school systems to our country.

This effort will be welcomed because unlike NCLB, it will not be viewed as an "intrusive pressure" or a "federal demand" but as federal *help* to actually crack the code of persistent schooling challenges that our cities and states struggle to solve. Also, it will not operate "outside" the current structure of public education or threaten the local control bias that currently exists. As will be described below, a critical part of the legislation will be to bring about these new designs first and foremost within existing public school systems.

This legislation will be timely because today, unlike fifteen years ago, there are serious private-sector education partners that can be called upon by the federal government to be a crucial part of this. While two decades ago the feds would have had almost nowhere to turn for assistance in the creation and launch of new schools in America, now they have perhaps a dozen entities that could be both designers and providers. They include players like Sylvan, Edison Schools, National Heritage Academies, the University of Phoenix, DeVry, the Broad Foundation, the Gates Foundation, and others. And if presented with the right opportunities, the entrepreneurs at companies not directly included in school management, such as McGraw-Hill and Pearson, might engage as well.

So what should this new act set out to accomplish?

At its core should be the dramatic expansion of federal educational research and development, with an emphasis on development. We must create an entity within education that is equivalent in scope to the NIH in health care—and equivalent in energy and creativity to the early days of NASA. This new function—let's nickname it ERD (educational R&D)—should be charged with three critical purposes: (1) a dramatic increase in both investment and the degree of innovation in whole-school design; (2) much greater investment in enhancing the critical "components" that go into successful schooling, such as mission-critical curriculum and training; and (3) the acceleration of greater supply, particularly of these new designs and components, within the limited "free markets" that now exist.

The creation of much more effective whole-school designs should be at the heart of this effort, but ERD should not limit its mission to this. More effective critical ingredients, components, and support systems will be needed by all those involved in these new whole-school designs. (The analogue here is that DoD doesn't just fund the creation of complete aircraft designs; it also funds innovation in critical components, such as new avionic suites, new forms of radar, new training techniques, and new air-traffic-control capabilities.) ERD would thus similarly fund critical research into the most advanced reading, math, and science curricula, how we should better motivate students, and how we should develop and educate school leaders and teachers. Just as the NIH has whole centers devoted to the cure of only one disease, so we should see R&D centers dedicated to critical components of the education experience. And at every turn, ERD's investments would be focused not on strictly academic research, but rather on development aimed specifically, directly, and decisively at producing measurable improvements in academic achievement.

As for bringing enhanced supply into existence, it is critical that the federal government and this new legislation recognize that as difficult and costly as it will be to develop breakthrough designs and components, *it will be more difficult for those designs to find their way into the marketplace of public education.* Aiding in their conception is important, *but seeing these new ideas through birth and infancy is equally so.* ERD must take an active and substantial role in incubating these designs in significant numbers so they can reach meaningful numbers of children and build the capacity to go beyond pilot stages. Perpetual pilot-project syndrome and incrementalism are the enemies of systematic reform. ERD must help break the barriers to widespread entry for these inventions or they will become nothing more than nice thoughts. Doing so will ensure not only new school concepts but the growth and development of important new provider organizations as well, an important "next step" in U.S. education history. ERD must view creating and nurturing large-scale providers as a strategic initiative critical to the country's future competitive position in the world.

Sometimes it is best to inform buyers of the costs of something before you actually show them what they will be receiving. It makes it easier for them to listen to what you are proposing. So before discussing what the specific programs of ERD might be for its first decade, let me give you an idea of what the costs would be.

Everything that is about to be recommended would cost the federal government $300 to $500 million per year in the first four years and about $4 billion per year in Years 5 through 15. To place this in some perspective, the initial $300–$500 million per year is about a 1 to 2 percent increase in current U.S. *federal* spending on schools, and a mere doubling or tripling of the anemic federal investment in education R&D. Four billion dollars per year, the "out years" number, is only 15 percent of what the feds currently spend on health care–related R&D—and less than 1 percent of the combined spending on K–12 education by local, state, and federal entities. The point? By national standards, these are relatively small sums that will accomplish, as you will see, a great deal. For American education, such an initiative would be an unprecedented, transformational, and historic action. And the return on this investment will affect the very health of our nation.

We can find that money one of two ways. Given that it is modest by federal standards, it could be new spending. But if we are in an era of frugality, it could simply be reprogrammed from existing educational spending at the federal level. This will create some howls, no doubt, but ask yourself this: If educational results have been flat for twenty years despite massive federal increases in spending, is reprogramming illogical?

Another important comment: The difference between research and development should be clearly understood. Research is examination, illumination, discovery—all critical aspects of innovation. Development is about making something workable, about bringing it to life and scale, often within a preexisting and relatively fixed economic reality. If research is seeing, development is doing. ERD's agenda must weight both equally. Why? Research without development, particularly in the world of schooling, will remain a document on a shelf, not affecting the lives of teachers and children. ERD must be not only about discovery *but also about the launch of its discoveries.*

If one must be given priority over the other, it should be development.

———

Here is what the legislation related to ERD should call for in its first-decade research-and-development agenda. It should consist of five major components:

Section I. The Creation and Launch of Three Major New K–12 School Designs and the Systems to Support Them

The first act of ERD would be to fund the creation and significant launch of three highly innovative K–12 school designs. To be quite specific, its objective might be for *each* of these three designs to serve approximately 330,000 children in 330 K–12 sites, beginning actual school operations by no later than 2010 and ramping up to the above target enrollment through the early part of the next decade. These three new designs would be serving about 1 million children by the middle of the next decade, or about 2 percent of U.S. schoolchildren. Though in percentage terms that number sounds small, it represents sufficient scale to be effective, noticeable, and relevant to the entire U.S. education community. In effect, the federal government would be calling for the creation of three new networks or systems of schools, *each* of which would rank in size in the top ten public school systems in the United States.

To begin, as Phase I, ERD would ask leading educational organizations in the United States to compete for three $150 million design and start-up grants. Incredibly modest sums by DoD standards, for instance. Each would be asked to create, over a period of three years from the issuance of the grant, new high-performance K–12 school designs and school-system designs (that is, simultaneous site and system designs), to include, but not be limited to, school organization and staffing models, schedules, professional-development programs, certain software applications, some curriculum, and the systems of support around all of these. Assuming 2007 passage of the act, the design grants would occur in 2007 with school openings scheduled for 2010. Though any organization could compete for the grant, my guess is that applicants would come from four major categories: (1) existing and significant schooling, preschooling, tutoring, or higher-education companies (University of Phoenix, DeVry, Edison, Sylvan, KinderCare, Kaplan, Princeton Review); (2) major nonprofits currently engaged in education reform (the Broad Foundation, the Gates Foundation, NewSchools Venture Fund, or any number of universities with schools of education); (3) companies involved in "components" of schools that are interested in entering the "whole-school market" (Harcourt, McGraw-Hill, Pearson, etc.); (4) major U.S. entities not currently involved in education per se, but with related expertise. (Two examples of the final category might be Disney, which knows much about how to communicate with children, and HCA, an organization that knows a great deal about running complex sites.) Intriguingly, consortia might well be formed between and within these categories to enhance capabilities and the likelihood of a winning entry.

Organizations would be chosen on the basis of two critical criteria: (1) their ability to create a powerful new design and (2) their ability to *execute* that design over the coming decades in 330 sites. In other words, ERD would be looking not only for "design capability" but for "production capacity" as well—the ability, so to speak, not just to design the plane but also to produce hundreds that actually fly.

The $150 million grant would be not only for creation of the design but also for the buildup of the systems that would be required to launch the design in the initial 330 sites. The design and system buildup would occur simultaneously, reducing the time to market by a significant number of years.

Those entities receiving the grants would be asked to create A and B models of their design. The A model would be a design that could be executed for exactly the same amount that we currently spend on American public education per pupil, annually adjusted for inflation. The B model would be a design that costs roughly 10 percent *more* than existing schools. The purpose of this is twofold. First, it ensures that the design will work within current economic realities—that these are not pipe-dream ideas, built on a prayer of massive new expenditures in K–12 in order to become a reality. Second, it puts into the marketplace designs that would demonstrate to policy makers what an additional 10 percent of educational funding could "buy" for our nation's schools.

Phase II of this would launch the designs into the marketplace. Each design provider would be required to launch three tranches of 110 schools each between 2011 and 2014. Half of the sites would be the lower-cost A models, and half of the sites would be the more expensive B models. (Though this ramp rate might sound ambitious, it is not unusual for significant multi-site organizations to launch hundreds of sites in their ramp-up years. Gap has opened over a hundred sites in one year; Home Depot has launched nearly two hundred annually; and Wal-Mart even today opens as many as two hundred huge installations annually. In fact, just *one* of America's fastest-growing school systems, Clark County, Nevada [Las Vegas], has been launching as many as thirteen new schools *per year* for over a decade, and that is in just one city.)

But how would these sites come about? Where would they be? Who would fund their launch capital? And most important, who would fund their annual operations? Herein lies the third leg of this stool, with ERD being one leg, the design providers being the second, and America's public school systems being the critical third partner.

Two-thirds of these new sites would be launched *in partnership* with America's existing public school systems. Why? Because a major objective of this effort would be to expose a large portion of America's educational community to the effectiveness of these new designs—and to the concept of working with alternative providers. Each provider would be required to "recruit" school districts that desired to try these new designs in their system of schools. And the federal government would provide incentives for districts to adopt these new schools. Districts would be asked to enter into twenty-year contracts with the providers to manage one or more schools under the new design. (If you think that is a long time, it is roughly equal to the length of time over which Boeing will produce the F-22.) The district would be responsible for providing the facility (from existing stock or through normal bond methods), while the design provider would completely manage the school under the new design. In the A model (existing-funds version), the school district would give the design provider the average annual amount it spends per child. And ERD would provide the school district with approximately $1,750 per child per year as an incentive to undertake this program—and an agreement that this per-pupil stipend would be in place for the twenty-year contract that the district signed with the provider. Why $1,750? The average U.S. school district receives $8,742 from local, state, and federal sources to educate a child. Typically, 25 percent of that supports the district's "infrastructure/support systems" and the other 75 percent goes to the schools. If a district were to adopt a new design from a provider and give the provider the entire per-pupil funding, then the district would lose the amount that had been supporting its infrastructure. It is precisely this problem that causes so many districts to resist new designs. And it is precisely this that makes the *$1,750 per year per child a critical element in bringing a great new supply of these new designs to America's educational markets.* In the past, even innovative districts, districts genuinely looking for better educational approaches, have been reluctant to adopt new designs, because, directly and indirectly, they force the districts to reduce their infrastructure, something they are reluctant to do, even if they no longer have to support the school being launched.

(Regarding the B models—the higher-spending ones—the feds would provide districts the annual extra per-pupil funds for these enriched designs in addition to the $1,750 per pupil noted above.)

In return for the federal "stipend," districts would be required to ensure that these new designs and providers were free to execute their design vigorously. This does not mean that these new schools would function without public oversight of taxpayer dollars or outside collective-bargaining agreements, but it does mean that the "nonfinancial" aspects of many of those agreements would need significant, even dramatic, modification.

While two-thirds of schools would operate within existing school systems, the other one-third would be set up as charter schools, meaning about 110 new charter schools for each design. As an incentive to cooperate, each participating state would be given a financial reward from ERD for its existing charter-school program. The purpose of this second group of schools, operating independently of districts, would be to determine if these new designs functioned better free of any district constraint. It would also send a message to any districts resistant to change: Allow these new designs and providers the freedom to flourish *within* your systems, or face the possibility that they could become competitors *outside your system* in years to come.

An important additional element that the ERD would provide for the charter group would be federal guarantees on facility bonds for these 330 schools. Assuming an average facility cost of about $15 million, this would mean federal enhancements on about $4.5 billion of school construction. That may sound large, but spread across many years it is a small portion of the U.S. school-construction budget. Further, given the very low rate of failure of significant charter schools, it is unlikely that more than a tiny fraction of the federal guarantee would ever be called.

You might ask why this should be done on such a significant scale. Why do we need three new designs? Why do we need a thousand of these new schools? Why not do just a few?

On the question of multiple designs, look at the NIH and how it is attacking cancer through myriad strategies. Just as there were many trails across the mountains during America's migration to the West, so it should be in the next frontier of school designs. We should diversify our research-and-development efforts and remember that there is no single answer to this (or any other) complex problem. We should also assume that one or more of these designs might not prove as valuable as we would like. To phrase it differently, we should have redundancy in something as critical as the creation of our next generation of schools.

As for why we should approach this with scale, it is important to understand that we are not creating just new schools *but new school systems*. As noted earlier, a 2003 Brookings research report showed that the best-gaining charter schools in America were connected to some type of system, not operating as islands. That should be no surprise to the serious student of school reform. The idea that great and *sustainably great* schools will spring up in large numbers from underfunded and unsupported efforts might be politically appealing, but it is organizational fantasyland. ERD's agenda should be the launch of a few systems, rather than the launch of a few sites. And for systems to be effective and efficient, they must have sufficient scale. A critical warning to any legislator considering this: *Lack of scale is a prescription for meaninglessness in the educational arena.* If you want this to work, you must commit to do it on a scale that will survive, that will persevere against resistance, that will command the attention of all, and that will have the strength to grow on its own following the initial assistance of the federal government. As a nation, we need to be serious here, not cute.

Think about what just this portion of the ERD agenda would yield. By 2020, America would have three completely new systems of schools in operation, each based on different designs and supported by different systems, each educating about 330,000 students, and each working with perhaps 100 or so public school systems scattered across the country. Together, they would be larger than the entire charter-school market today. These designs would be of an entirely different quality from what we now see in isolated school districts and unsupported charter schools or even early networks of charter schools. Each of these three systems would be operated by provider entities that would, by 2020, have revenues of about $3 billion annually from these initial networks. In today's dollars, this would place them roughly in the Fortune 1000. Each would dwarf any current provider's reach and scale. Not only would ERD have been responsible for putting new designs into America's educational marketplace, but it would have also led the way in taking capacity to a new plateau. That capacity is an essential building block. From there, these providers could fund much more of their own R&D as they expand beyond the initial 330 sites. Each would begin approaching districts to expand its designs further. The best of the designs, determined by student results, would grow faster, and that is just as it should be. And these major new providers would do something else: they would begin repaying ERD its initial R&D grants through royalties, with those new revenues to ERD funding additional R&D efforts in the years ahead. ERD should have some "intellectual property benefits" from what it helped create.

Think about how it would impact a typical American city. As an example, scattered about the Denver metroplex in several different school districts and as charters might be ten of these new schools, two or three from each provider. Though they might educate directly only 3 to 5 percent of the students in the region, every district would be thinking about whether it should contract for more of these new designs.

As ambitious as this is, ERD should not stop here. There is much more to do. ERD must think not only in terms of the whole but also in terms of the parts—the critical components, the sensitive and perhaps rare raw materials.

Section II. Design and Launch of New Principal Universities

In Chapter 6, the importance of great principals was emphasized. The nation cannot leave the supply of these indispensable individuals to chance. If uranium is the critical fuel in a nuclear power plant, then principals are the uranium of our schools. The country must view the continued supply of principals as a strategic issue, just as we have done with critical raw materials in other sectors. We must develop "strategic reserves" of these individuals. And this work, the work of enhancing supply alternatives, should be done through ERD, again with private-sector partners. In time, as discussed earlier in this book, major alternative providers will develop their own principal colleges or universities. But the nation should not wait for that to happen. In Chapter 6, we proposed the creation of new federally backed "principal universities," the equivalents of our Air Force Academy, West Point, and Annapolis. Here we talk about how this should be part of ERD's research-and-development agenda.

The development of these new institutions might occur in six steps:

Step One: In 2007, ERD would specifically call for the creation of these universities.

Step Two: ERD would then put out a "request for proposals" to create five new national principal universities. Companies, foundations, and universities, or consortia among them, would make "initial proposals," due in early 2008, to create new multiyear graduate programs for principals.

Step Three: ERD might select ten finalists from all the initial applicants and provide each with $10 million in design fees, giving them one year to complete their final proposals.

Step Four: In 2008, ERD would select a diverse group of providers (example: two universities, two companies, and one foundation) to create and build the new colleges or universities, located strategically around the United States. This ensures multiple designs and both nonprofit and for-profit approaches. Each entity might be given $15 million of start-up loans and federal credit enhancements of $100 million to build five approximately 600,000-square-foot complexes of classroom facilities and residences, each for approximately 3,000 students.

Step Five: The five universities could open in 2011 or 2012 with Year 1 classes of 1,000, growing to full capacity over the next two years. The five new facilities would supply a substantial portion of the United States's annual principal needs at that point.

Step Six: Under the same act, ERD could provide $30,000 per year in student loans to cover anticipated full tuition and expenses of students.

For $100 million in design fees, $75 million in start-up loans, credit enhancements for campus construction, and an increase in its current student loan program, the federal government could dramatically enhance school leadership in the United States. Another important warning for legislators regarding these important institutions: As is often the case, there will be a legislative tendency to spread the wealth—to put one in every state. *Resist that temptation.* The result will be fifty watered-down projects, not five transforming institutions. It would be like saying, "Instead of West Point or the Air Force Academy, let's leave the development of our country's military leadership institutions to fifty National Guards." Wrong plan. It is critical to focus and concentrate resources in order to bring about the change we need.

ERD will have a much larger universe of providers to choose from for this mission than for the school-design mission. Top universities will compete vigorously. K–12 school operators, already deeply involved in the development of school leadership, will see this as a natural, vertical-integration extension of their core business, just as the hypothetical schooling companies earlier in this book did. Certain foundations, particularly those already investing in school leadership programs, such as the Broad Foundation, may choose to compete. And finally, heavyweights of the for-profit higher-education world—the University of Phoenix, DeVry, and others—will probably step up, seeing this as a diversification of their current offerings. If you believe competition brings out the best in us, ERD should find itself with a superb and exciting group of options here, too. And more important, from this will grow the equivalent of our great military academies in education.

The same competitors may find the next portion of ERD's agenda equally interesting.

Section III. The Creation of Five New Teacher Colleges

There are those who believe that America's teacher colleges are part of the problem of our K–12 system. We'll leave that to others to debate. What is not debatable, however, is that we need to push the envelope in the development of our teachers. And here ERD can play a pivotal role.

The number of new school leaders to be trained per year is relatively small. ERD can thus move quickly and directly to create a handful of important institutions that will largely provide the country with the school leadership it needs. On the teacher front, we need about *250,000* new teachers per year, a wholly different issue of scale. Today, over 1,200 colleges provide America's annual teacher needs. Here, ERD cannot directly solve the supply issue, but it should lead the way in innovation, bringing to market new designs for teacher education, innovation that one would hope will be followed by other colleges and universities that wish to compete with these new lead entities.

As called for by the new legislation, ERD would ask companies, foundations, and universities to compete to create ten new substantial teacher colleges, again strategically placed across the country. The act would call for ERD to approach this on a timetable similar to that of the principal universities and through similar competitive procedures—design grants, requests for proposals, and so on.

Section IV.
Critical-Components Research

No matter what whole-school designs come out of Section I of ERD's research agenda, every design will require certain crucial components that can be best developed by highly specialized entities separate and apart from the whole-school designers. In its own literature, the current highly limited federal research program within IES says it has "a persuasive research program" in only one critical component: reading. The Education Innovation Act of 2007 should dramatically expand that reading research program and add robust development programs for several other areas as well. Again, ERD should seek out entities that can both conduct the research for these components and bring the results of that research quickly to market (no later than 2010) in product form: usable curriculum and related training. In each critical arena ERD should make research-and-development grants to two competitive entities to ensure that multiple methods come to market. Specifically, the act should require grants of $50 million to $150 million in each arena. The critical arenas would be:

A. **Student-Motivation Programs.** As noted in the chapter on new school design, finding ways to draw out the natural, built-in motivations of children should be a major ingredient of new designs. ERD should fund the development of such programs, whose results will be felt in every area of achievement.

B. **No-Failure-Accepted Reading and Math Programs.** America needs curricula and protocols that ensure literacy and numeracy for 99.9 percent of our children. NCLB requires states to achieve this by 2014. Should we not help them find the best tools? We should approach reading and math curricula the same way we approach vaccination: they should work *virtually all the time.*

C. **New Science Programs.** If America is going to compete successfully against emerging economies in the coming century, our schools must be able to train world-class scientists. ERD should be in the forefront of research not only on how to teach children science but also on how to attract them to the field early in their lives.

D. **Core Life-Skills Programs.** Everything from learning to use computers, to research techniques, to learning how to speak and make presentations, to understanding how the world of work actually functions is largely left to chance in our schools today or given very small resources. In most cases these are add-ons or handled by organizations outside the scope of the school. Particularly at the high school level, these should be integral parts of school design.

E. **Character Education and Discipline Systems.** As with core skills, character education and the discipline systems of our schools are left largely to the individual creativity of teachers and school staff. Sometimes this works brilliantly—and sometimes it works not at all. The ethical development of our children is surely a national concern, and we should not leave it to chance.

F. **Effective Second-Language Programs.** The next time you are with a group of people, ask these two questions: (1) Did you take a foreign language in school? and (2) Can you now speak it fluently? The answer to the first question will be almost 100 percent yes—and the answer to the second will probably be less than 10 percent yes, showing virtually a 90 percent failure rate of schools to bring our students to second-language fluency. In the past, perhaps this was acceptable; perhaps we could, as a nation, "get away with it." Perhaps we've been operating on the premise that everyone else in the world had to learn our language, as we have been the world's lead dog. Put aside the arguable arrogance of that and ask whether it is prudent for us to continue under that assumption as we go through this century. ERD programs on how to get high percentages of our children to fluency in other languages could pay major dividends in the decades ahead. And we're probably not talking about the old standbys, French and German. Think Chinese and Hindi—and one old standby, Spanish.

Section V. The Creation of School-System "Platforms"

As previously discussed, the NIH and those receiving its grants do not attack a particular disease or opportunity from one angle. They pursue multiple strategies simultaneously, unclear as to which one will ultimately prove most successful. So it should be with the world of schools.

In Sections I through IV of the ERD research agenda, I have suggested that America approach the improvement of our schools from four angles: new school designs, creation of new leadership capacity, better development of our teacher corps, and spurring innovation in critical components. All these are "bottom-up" strategies—starting at the school level or the "component level." There is another strategy that is more district-based in its approach: the creation of "system platforms," or "system suites."

As noted in earlier chapters, America's school systems are, when compared with other sectors of the American economy, incredibly fragmented. There are nearly 15,000 school systems out there, each with an average of only six schools. Each of those systems is struggling with the myriad problems that any school system must deal with, including (1) school designs, (2) professional development of leaders and teachers, (3) curriculum choices, (4) assessment systems, (5) information systems, (6) technology platforms, (7) school construction and maintenance, and (8) recruitment of staff. These are just examples; the full list stretches far beyond. Each district is "making" some of these things, "buying" others, and trying to integrate them into an effective and efficient system. To be blunt, each is hopelessly stretched in trying to do so. Even the largest district lacks the scale to take on all these tasks.

So what do we do? One approach would simply be to combine thousands of districts. Any politician reading this just laughed out loud, knowing the chance of getting thousands of school districts to consolidate anytime in the next three centuries is about as remote as putting the Soviet Union back together again. But there might be a better way, a way in which districts maintain their independence and local governance but opt, voluntarily, toward a future that utilizes the advantage of scale. Middleburg, Tennessee, supposedly followed this scenario in Chapter 8. It is an approach that the ERD research agenda must include.

Imagine a time in the future when a district had a choice between several completely integrated education platforms. In other words, imagine that a handful of companies developed an integrated suite of systems and services that a district could purchase as a whole, rather than trying to cobble together a bunch of unrelated capabilities that were not built with a whole in mind. Imagine, for example, that a company came to a district with something like this offer: "We'll do the following things for you as a package. We'll bring you reading, math, and science programs. We'll recruit your teachers and principals (we bring the candidates; you decide if you like them). We'll provide all your professional development, completely integrated into your curriculum selections. We'll provide a seamless technology and information system, including real-time assessment and advance information systems. We'll provide your financial planning systems (though you will decide what your budgets will be). We'll help design your reward systems. And we'll be doing this with hundreds, perhaps thousands, of other school districts around the country, using that expertise and scale to do everything we do for you very well, and very cost-efficiently."

Some might ask what the *district* does if another entity is responsible for all that. Plenty, as was described earlier in the Middleburg hypothetical example. The district would be the accountable manager on all personnel matters. It would manage all collective-bargaining arrangements. The district would create and manage the physical infrastructure of the school system. The district would control the finances of the system. It would be the interface with the community itself. And don't forget, it would hire and fire the platform provider. In short, the district would be the boss.

The message of the company providing this would be to join a national network of school systems, each operating off a similar platform. Just as local television stations are affiliates of national networks, yet remain independent and are locally owned, and just as local newspapers use the major wire services of national news operations, yet do their own reporting as well, so it could be with school systems of the future.

ERD should foster the creation of these new platforms. One approach would be to require the companies competing for the school-design grants in Section I of this agenda to *also* develop a platform of their systems to offer to *smaller* school districts across the United States. If ERD elected to go this way, it would be important to offer these districts transition funds to move from their old systems to these new platforms. Ultimately, the new platforms should cost roughly the same as the current "cobbled-together" ones. But the "change-out costs" could be substantial in the early years. The ERD role could be twofold: (1) jump-starting the creation of these platforms; and (2) assisting districts in their transition to them. A quick estimate of what those transition costs might be is $1.5 million per year for an average U.S. school system (about 5 percent of an average school-system budget). ERD might provide 1,000 smaller and rural districts with ten-year transition grants to these platforms, beginning with $1.5 million per year per district and ramping down throughout the course of the ten years. This would encourage districts to make the leap to the next world—and give companies incentive to enter the market.

For members of Congress who come from rural states, this portion of the research agenda should be very important. It is hard enough for major-city school systems to afford the system development that our schools will require in the century ahead. To ask this of the thousands of districts in America that have only a few schools is completely unrealistic.

To conclude this chapter, imagine the news coverage in 2007 if the federal government actually did something like this. I'm betting they might call it the most important legislation since Social Security, the most creative since NASA. A particularly creative newspaper might dub it "Homeland Offense."

If I were to imagine what quotes from legislative sponsors might be, here is what I would guess: "For decades we've known that our schools were not performing as we would like," said cosponsoring Senators Edward Kennedy, D-Mass., and Lamar Alexander, R-Tenn., in an unusual joint statement. "We've sent them money. We've raised the bar on state tests. We've scolded and embarrassed them. Today we've done something very different. We're setting in motion a process to provide dramatic new solutions to their problems. No more nibbling at the edges. As a nation, we've been doing this in the health care arena for nearly a century. It is about time that we invested in our minds as much as our bodies."

EPILOGUE:
LETTERS TO LEADERS

This period of time is an important moment in the movement that Edison leads. I've learned that the world of schools is faddish. To a fault, it is an arena that likes, even requires, new ideas, understandably preferring a new flavor of the month to the sometimes tedious implementation of a good idea over a long period of time against persistent adversity. American education is capable of rejecting promising approaches even in their infancy simply to look for a new "bumper-sticker" solution to the endlessly reported woes of our schools. Our public schools are politically managed, and political managers need fresh red meat to fuel their reelection or sustain their appointment. Private involvement in public schools—though, truthfully, still in its infancy—is, by political standards, an "old idea." It runs the risk of being labeled "Oh, we did that years ago" when it is on the verge of its most exciting years. Part of the purpose of this book is to keep that phenomenon from setting in, to let policy makers and press lords know that just as Mars missions take decades, real change in schools takes decades, too. It is important that we all see this mission through to its landing. It is important that we all take leadership roles in supporting the next phase. It is important, most of all, that we truly understand what has happened and what will happen in the future.

In the preceding chapters, I have done my best to show the powerful facts and, I hope, clear logic that point to where we need to go to improve American schools and how we best can get there.

But making these changes will hinge on so much more than facts and logic. It will require real people, working under complex and conflicting pressures, to make choices to do the hard work of getting there. In many instances, key players will need to set aside painful professional experiences and personal animosities to work with adversaries and rivals to create a new future for American education.

Political insiders say, "Don't let anyone fool you: politics is personal. Very personal." I thus am concluding this book with a personal plea to some of the people who will have much to say about whether or not our schools become great. Some are my friends or natural allies. Some are my adversaries or consider themselves natural enemies of the ideas presented here. All will have considerable impact on whether or not these ideas move forward.

Each of these letters has already been sent, along with a copy of this book, prior to its publication. I have no doubt that some of the recipients will genuinely disagree with some of my arguments. Others will feel obliged to do so. My hope is that they will engage on these matters nonetheless.

The stakes could not be higher. Our nation's leadership in the world hangs in the balance.

Mr. Ed McElroy
President
American Federation of Teachers
Washington, D.C.

Mr. Reg Weaver
President
National Education Association
Washington, D.C.

Ms. Randi Weingarten
President
United Federation of Teachers
New York, N.Y.

Dear Ed, Reg, and Randi:

I write to you because you are important leaders in America's
union movement. Ed and Randi, I have had the pleasure of
knowing and working with you over the years. Reg, although I
have not yet had the opportunity to work with you, I look forward to doing so.

Your decisions, and those of the thousands of heads of union
locals around the country, will determine in significant measure the shape and speed of the events described in this book. No
other educational organizations have the power and scope of the
NEA, the AFT, and their thousands of local affiliates. That is
true, in no small measure, because your organizations long ago
embraced three central premises of this book: (1) the power of
scale, (2) the importance of merging scale with the qualities of
local control, and (3) the criticality of continuity of leadership.

Union locals are independent and determine their own courses of action, but they are hugely supported by their national organizations. As I have noted in my book, I often joke that unions are the only pro teams on the field of play in education—and that a confrontation between a school board and a union local is typically the equivalent of the Packers playing a local high school team. One way to view it is to contrast the annual dues of the NEA and AFT with the entire annual budget of an average school board. This is not a criticism of unions. It is a compliment to their organizational prowess.

Similarly, at both the local and national levels, unions are typically the long-term players. Albert Shanker was head of the AFT for over twenty years, a tenure unheard of in major superintendencies. The power and perspective that emerge from such a length of duty are not to be underestimated. And it is true at the local level as well. More often than not, the presidents of union locals serve far longer than their school board or superintendent counterparts. Case in point: Adam Urbanski, head of the AFT in Rochester, New York, has worked with six superintendents during his tenure. In most cities, the union is the true institutional memory of the educational enterprise.

Other than government itself, America's teacher unions are the most important players in American education. No other organizations in education have their national scope, their political budgets, or their sheer manpower. Though some (myself included) may disagree with your positions on certain issues (as you do with mine), they cannot take away your persistence, your organizational strength, and the important benefits you have brought to your membership. All of which is to say that on all matters important, unions have a very large seat at the educational table. With respect for that position I ask for your support of the vision laid out in this book. I know that is a significant request, something that will not be easy for you to give.

Some of your members will roll out the privatization bogeyman, saying this is privatization writ large. I hope you will conclude, as I believe, that nothing in this book proposes any such thing. Privatization is, according to one dictionary, "the conversion of a public enterprise to a private enterprise. For example, a government-owned railroad or airline may undergo privatization if ownership shares of the enterprise are sold to individual and institutional investors." I propose nothing of that sort. (A national voucher system, on the other hand, could well fit that description.)

Others will pound their fists about the immorality of profits in the classroom. Putting aside that Edison is clearly not a get-rich-quick scheme (having made no profits in thirteen of its fourteen years!), I would respectfully argue that this is also a diversionary argument. If profits cannot be made in education, then here is a partial list of things that should be removed from schools immediately: textbooks, computers, desks, milk, pencils, paper, and all athletic supplies and uniforms. And let's not forget to tear all school buildings down! Virtually every one was built by a for-profit contractor. We will have to untrain millions of teachers, too, because much of the professional development they have received was conducted by for-profit concerns. Let's say it bluntly: Whether a profit is made or not should not be the litmus test of whether a policy is good or bad. That test should be *results for children and, yes, teachers*. If a firm can make a margin while delivering higher marks, what tenet in our nation's culture and values says that is wrong? And here is something indisputably true: there will be no earning without learning, certainly not in the long term. If firms don't deliver academic results, there will not be, and should not be, any escape from the consequences (or the harsh floodlight of the media). You will call for such firms to be fired. You will be right to do so. And they will be—just as Edison has been fired when we have not delivered.

No doubt there will be an outcry from some of your leadership regarding one particular part of this book that proposes fewer but much-higher-paid teachers in the future. Some will scream, "Many of you are going to be fired." That is not true, and I hope you will discourage the use of that shorthand. The changes I advocate would take years to roll out nationally, and no teacher would lose his or her job as a result—that is, any adjustment in total teaching positions could be easily managed through teacher attrition and/or growth in the number of children served. As you know better than I, the country as a whole will need to hire a sizable number of new teachers (by some estimates, over 2 million) in the next decade. I am simply advocating that as a nation we hire fewer of that number and pay them and everyone remaining much more.

Finally, some within your organizations will dismiss the entire thesis of this book as fantasy and attack me for doing it. They will say, "Yeah, Whittle said Edison would have an enrollment of a million students by now, and they are only serving 270,000 kids, not all of them full-time! This is never going to happen. Don't worry about it. They'll go broke soon enough. And their schools aren't that good anyway." When this response comes up, here is how you might privately respond to *them.* "Yes, Whittle's earlier predictions were not precise, but were they, perhaps, more accurate than ours? Didn't some in our organization say a decade ago that there would be *no* real private-sector involvement in education? Aren't nearly 15 percent of the public school students in D.C. in charters, most run by private entities? Did not the head of the Philadelphia district, a union-friendly Democrat, just predict that half of the schools in the eighth-largest district in the country would soon be in some type of private management? Isn't a Labour government in the U.K. spearheading substantial private-sector engagement in public schools? Doesn't Sweden, about as left-leaning a society as you will ever find, now have a national voucher system? Whittle was wrong on some things, but are we so sure we were right? More important, while predictions of the future are rarely exactly on target, is Whittle describing a trend that is happening here, one that we can't just dismiss? Might we do better to engage with it than to deny it?"

Privatizing! Profiteering! It will cost you your job! These will be the bumper stickers and slogans against what I am proposing, but you and I both know that there will be a much more important, much more private, discussion about this at the highest levels of your organizations. And that debate will be mainly on this topic: If this approach to public education were to play out, would that be a good thing or a bad thing for unions themselves? Would this potentially impair the well-being, the power, and the future of your organizations? Some idealists would say this should not even be a question, that the welfare of children should be paramount. That's easy for them to say, and unfair as well. Who is to say that an organization should not protect itself? And who says that the future of unions and the well-being of children are mutually exclusive? I don't.

So what is the answer to this key question? How would the thesis of this book impact your movement? It is likely to be found in two important subquestions: First, if powerful new private entities emerge, does that somehow, de facto, minimize or damage the role of unions? Ask it another way: Does the highly fragmented structure that now exists favor the power and influence of your organizations? Second, if America had fewer teachers per school than it has now, but they were paid much more, would that, per se, weaken the AFT and the NEA?

At first glance, it might seem that neither of these phenomena are pluses for your organizations. If you are currently kings and queens of the hill, which you are, why would you want the emergence of powerful new entities? And second, how could fewer teachers possibly be a positive?

Let's take first the question of fewer teachers. From a financial standpoint, this could well be a plus for the unions. If you presume that you increase dues as pay increases, then the impact on your gross revenues should be neutral. This assumption should particularly hold true if you choose to be at the forefront of the changes that bring that pay raise about. Then, when extended to your cost structure, it becomes a net financial positive. If you have fewer teachers to serve but the same gross revenues, your "cost to serve" (as we say in the business world) should decline dramatically. Another example is that you might have substantially fewer bargaining agreements to manage. For instance, it is possible that you might have bargaining-agreement templates with each of the educational providers, templates that districts in "affiliate agreements" and their corresponding locals could easily modify. These savings could allow you to use those dollars for other important union initiatives, such as extending your political networks, enhancing your public advocacy, deepening your member services, and even improving resources for union staff members (which would be completely appropriate if the trends in teacher pay materialize as hoped). In effect, the union's "operating margin" should improve dramatically under the structure proposed here.

I must acknowledge that the fewer-teachers scenario is negative for you politically. It has often been said that teachers are the ground forces of American politics, and particularly of the Democratic Party. (I remember a Southern governor saying to me many years ago: "There's only one thing you have to know about politics in my state. Every teacher has every summer before every election off," meaning they could be part of the campaign during summer vacation.) If you believe part of your power is your ability to mobilize teacher votes, then I must concede that the approach I am advocating is a negative for the union. So as you weigh the pros and cons of this, put that one in the con column. But on the other side of the ledger, please note that you will probably have many more dollars to work with politically to offset the reduction in feet on the ground.

Now to the tougher question: Is it a good thing for unions to have other powerful entities in the world of education, ones that could, for example, have lobbying budgets approaching or even eventually exceeding your own? Does this somehow disturb the balance of power in a way that could be negative to your interests?

In a static world of education—that is, one that stays largely as it currently is—I can imagine no advantage to the unions in seeing new powers emerge. But I would respectfully argue that the analysis is more complex than that. What odds do you place that the world of schooling is not going to change in some major way over the next three decades? Can the world's leading nation, increasingly faced with serious world competition, maintain that leadership if it continues to doom 30 percent of its population to near illiteracy? Said plainly: Something's got to give. It is just a question of how and when. There is going to be some type of fundamental realignment. It seems to me that those in charge of the next era will be those who lead and shape the change of the current one—and those out of power or in weakened positions will be those who resist it. If this were a military situation, a general would say that the current position is, in the long term, simply indefensible. "There may be risk in moving," he would say, "but there is no risk at all in staying put. We will be defeated."

You know there are true enemies of unions, people who would like to place the problems of schools squarely on your doorstep. You know that NAEP scores have been more or less flat for two decades despite huge spending increases and that the achievement gap between children of color and white children is actually growing. All this argues that "change is a-comin'." The question is: Will you bring it about?

I have attempted in this letter to respond to things I know you will hear and to consider some of the strategic realities that I presume you must face. But I'd like to end on a different note: to make a case to you on why what I am proposing is good for teachers, children, and public education itself.

The Pentagon was recently criticized for not providing American troops with sufficient armor on Humvees. Our country is doing something far worse to its teachers. We send them into classrooms every day without the tools they need, without the training they should have, and without all sorts of "air cover" that would make them more successful. And, for sure, they don't get combat pay. When, inevitably, the results of these omissions are not what we want, most of the attention is focused on the tragedy this entails for children, as it should be. But what happens to teachers? You know all too well that the casualties here are not just children but also the hundreds of thousands of teachers who leave their chosen field quickly because they cannot find a way to succeed. And that doesn't count the hundreds of thousands more who stay but don't feel as good as they might about what they are doing. What I'm advocating in this book is designed, straight up, to address these endemic problems. Teachers in schools of the future would have far greater support, much better tools, better information, and much higher pay. If the well-being of teachers is paramount to your organizations, as I know it is, could we not find a way to work together to bring it about?

Though teachers are your primary constituency, I know that your organizations care deeply about children, too. How could it be otherwise, given that you are organizations of teachers, most of whom came to this field for that very reason? I'm convinced this book's vision will take our children to a new level of achievement. That's not just wishful thinking. I urge you to carefully study the recent RAND report on Edison's first decade and the most recent results from Philadelphia. These gains can be brought to children throughout the country and the world.

Last, you know better than most that public education itself is under attack. Although there are aspects of the approach I am advocating that you might not like, I hope you will compare those with other strategies being proposed elsewhere that, for all practical purposes, would eliminate public education in America. This book proposes a way that our schools can continue to be public and continue to be under the control of democratically controlled institutions.

I suppose my argument for your support boils down to this: Maintenance of the status quo is not only untenable but unthinkable. In that context, it is not whether change is going to occur but what change it is going to be. I believe the evolution proposed in this book embraces the union movement, while others would choose to destroy it.

Sincerely,
Chris Whittle

Editors of *The New York Times, The Wall Street Journal, USA Today*
Editors of *Time* and *Newsweek*
News Producers of ABC, NBC, CBS, CNN, and Fox

Dear Editors and Producers:

Each of you holds a unique and powerful perch. Together, you are the three largest national papers, the five largest news networks, and the two largest newsweeklies. Not only do you reach, over the course of a week, a majority of the American public, but each of you in your own way is a journalistic leader held in respect by media throughout the country. Together, you have earned positions of great sway over both Americans and the American media.

My hope is that you will expose your readers to some of the thoughts developed here. If you have read this far and are considering coverage, then there are some journalistic questions you might have already asked. First, is there really news here? Or is this just refried beans, something that has already been covered, even years ago? Second, if you deem this to be newsworthy, then what kind of news is it? Should you assign an education writer/producer, a political one, a business one? And third, if you are going to take an editorial position, in particular on the legislative agenda proposed herein, what should be your point of view?

On the question "Is this news?" you will have to be the judges, but I can perhaps help out by telling you some things this book is not. This is not about charter schools. It is also not about privatization or vouchers. It is not a right-wing or a left-wing plot. This is fundamentally about a new way for America to (1) design its schools and (2) approach the structure of public education, both growing in part from things I have learned as one of the longest-serving "superintendents" in public education today.

On the question of what kind of story it is, there I might be able to help. The topics presented here sit squarely at the intersection of education, politics, and business. And that means, should you choose to cover it, you'll need either one very broad-gauged reporter or a team drawn from your different disciplines.

If you decide to take an editorial position one way or another, I hope you'll think about urging federal legislators to increase this country's research-and-development funding and agenda in education. It may be unrealistic to ask them to provide education the same federal commitment to R&D that we find in health care ($27 billion from the feds each year versus less than $270 million for education), but you might want to urge them to increase spending dramatically.

Finally, if you should find yourself in a position to support some or all of what is said in *Crash Course,* please refrain from simultaneously condemning public educators for our current results. The effect of such an attack is to alienate them from the solutions proposed here. This is a phenomenon I've seen again and again over the years, where reporters, thinking privately that they are helping to drive reform, actually polarize the situation by saying, effectively, "Look how much better this is than what we now have." It's a mistake I have also made.

Thank you for your consideration.

Sincerely,
Chris Whittle

School Board Members, K–12 Districts
c/o Anne Bryant, Executive Director,
  National School Boards Association
School Superintendents, K–12 Districts
c/o Paul Houston, Executive Director,
  American Association of School Administrators

Dear District Officials:

Your reactions to the multiprovider and affiliate-agreement models and new school designs presented in this book could well be, at once, both excitement and concern. After all, what is being proposed here is far from business as usual.

Let's start with a key issue you will probably have to confront if you choose to move toward a multiprovider or an affiliate-agreement model, whether you come from a small or large district. Let's label it "the organizational-pride" issue.

There are going to be those within your district who will view what is proposed here as a giant step backward for the district and for public education itself. (Even you might have some of these feelings!) Whether they say it out loud or not, this is what they may be thinking: "This is an abdication of our responsibility. Doing anything like this is effectively an admission of our own failure. We should be doing these things ourselves. There's no reason we can't do this. Why bring in all these outsiders? We're not going to have as much control as we do now."

One way to confront those thoughts is with alternative images from other sectors that have had decades of partnerships, outsourcings, and collaborations. The Department of Defense does not feel that it has lost control when it subcontracts the building of a nuclear sub to a major defense contractor. Hundreds of corporations don't feel that they have abdicated their responsibility when they subcontract with EDS to run large parts of their data-processing system. NASA does not feel that it has failed in its mission because it works closely with the Jet Propulsion Laboratory to manage significant portions of its space missions. A homeowner does not feel a sense of loss when he turns to an architect and a general contractor to build his home. In each case, the "controlling party" was simply looking for the best way to get something done, accepting that others might have greater resources, experience, and expertise to tackle particular aspects of execution. And in every case, the credit for success rightly belonged to them, the boss. It was ultimately the homeowner's home, the Navy's sub, and NASA's mission, no matter who might have helped make it happen.

Which leads to an important corollary point: when one is bringing in partners, subcontractors, and collaborators, it is critical that the district *take credit for doing so.* After all, the district had the vision to bring in these resources, and the district will manage them and guide them to success. If you feel that it is abdication, you will not celebrate it, own it, and receive from it the credit you should. Embrace it! Be the first on the podium to say that you brought it to your constituents. You will have done so. It is only fair that you be recognized for this accomplishment.

But in addition to showing your staff successful partnership examples from other arenas, it will also be important for you to pierce organizational denial, wishful thinking, not-invented-here reactions, and the like. If your technology department walked in and said, "Hey, we've decided to build our own computers rather than buy them from Apple or Dell," you would quickly dismiss the suggestion with "That's not what we do best." You would have said the same if your building maintenance department had said, "A bunch of us in maintenance think we're going to build the new high school ourselves, rather than give it to a major contractor." In the times ahead, you will be called upon to make similar judgments, albeit ones that are more difficult, because the judgments ahead, at least in the beginning, will be less clear-cut, more nuanced, and more pioneering. Ahead, you will not be discussing buildings, computers, textbooks, or buses. You'll be talking about instruction, school design, professional development, recruitment, and assessment systems, to mention just a few. Traditionally, these have been largely off-limits to anyone but district personnel. These have been things "we do ourselves." Moving to external providers on these will test your leadership capability because resistance will be higher.

Fortunately, as you lead your district into the new educational structures of the future, you will have the excitement of a new order of things on your side. If the feeling of threat described above is the yin of change, then the yang is the rush felt when engaging in something new, something we intuit and hope could be far better than a reality we've grown weary of and know doesn't work as well as we would like. The pioneers and revolutionaries of your district will rally to these new concepts and relish the opportunities they represent. They will see this not as a threat but as something to harness. Your leading them to that place, your being the first out of the trench of the old, will release their energy and confidence. No one will be more grateful than your greatest achievers.

Finally, please do not wait for the changes described here to knock on your door. This critical evolution will begin when one or two or three districts *in every state* take the helm as its architects, its lead change agents. Don't wait for the developing schooling entities to come to you. Pick those that you think are going to emerge as the strongest and become their earliest partners in shaping this change.

When you do, I will happily join those who salute your vision.

Regards,
Chris Whittle

The Honorable Senator Edward Kennedy (D-Mass.)
The Honorable Senator Barack Obama (D-Ill.)

Dear Senators Kennedy and Obama:

I write to the two of you because you represent both the core values and the new vision of the Democrat Party; because you are wisdom and youth, white and black. Senator Kennedy, you have shown your courage on the matter of schools in cosponsoring the No Child Left Behind Act, while Senator Obama, you come from a city that knows all too well that children of color have been left behind for decades.

I ask that each of you support the federal legislative agenda proposed in Chapter 9 of this book. There are three good reasons to do so: the children of this country; not just the survival, but the strengthening of public education in America; and the future health of the Democratic Party. On the first two, I've already made my case in this book, and I hope you'll consider it carefully. On the third, please let me respectfully make a case to you both.

First, some disclosure about my personal politics. I am an independent. Sometimes I vote for Democrats, sometimes for Republicans. I have no ideological ax to grind. I provide advice and support to candidates of both parties on matters related to education. I support a wide range of educational choice for parents. I think NCLB is largely on the mark.

As you well know, there are those who believe that Republicans are gaining ground or, in fact, have seized the strategic heights on the issue of education. Two key reform items have been central to their educational platform. Choice, primarily in charter schools and secondarily in the voucher movement, has been largely Republican-backed. And the embodiment of accountability, NCLB, although enthusiastically supported by you, Senator

Kennedy, and by many Democrats, was proposed by a Republican administration. This is not to say that some Democrats have not backed both these movements, but rather that support has often been understandably lukewarm, given that the public education establishment, traditionally a Democratic stronghold, has not been, shall we say, wildly enthusiastic about many aspects of choice and accountability.

Choice and accountability are only two legs of a legislative stool that desperately needs a third. A choice with no place to go is meaningless. And choice in which the public schools cannot compete does nothing more than drain away enrollment in our public schools, which, like you, I believe to be one of our nation's most important institutions. Similarly, holding public education accountable without providing it with the tools needed to succeed could well be nothing more than a setup for failure. This is why it is so important for this nation and our federal government to bring about a third measure: the introduction of large amounts of *supply* of new and better schools, again something I have detailed extensively in Chapter 9 of this book. It is with this initiative that the Democratic Party could and should maintain a strong educational footing.

It will not be easy for you to do so. The initiatives outlined in this book will lead to a dramatic expansion of private entities within the education sector—entities that, ultimately, will be financially strong, politically influential, and global in reach. Some of your traditional supporters, particularly unions and some employees of public education systems, will view this as threatening. Some in your party will say it does nothing but create another business to back Republicans.

This, I would respectfully submit, is the moment for political wisdom and long-sightedness. You can show them that this new era need not be something to fear. You can convince them that the greater threat is holding on to a past that has so clearly failed so many of the children of precisely those constituents the Democratic Party was founded to help. And you can lead them to the view that strength will come from ownership of the future, not begrudging and late-to-the-party acceptance of it.

I am similarly calling upon the Republican Party to play an equal role in this next step in the resurgence of our public schools. Just as our children have mothers and fathers, they should have the support of both parties.

Thank you for listening.

Chris Whittle

Nevada Governor Kenny Guinn
    Chairman, Republican Governors Association
New Mexico Governor Bill Richardson
    Chairman, Democratic Governors' Association

Dear Governors Guinn and Richardson:

In 1992 I addressed the National Governors' Conference in Princeton, New Jersey. The idea of a national system of schools was then viewed as revolutionary, and governors wanted to hear about Edison's progress. After the speech, Governors John Engler (R-Mich.) and Roy Romer (D-Col.) essentially invited Edison to their states. With the governors' support, we launched schools in both states early in our formative period.

Governors will play an equally pivotal role in bringing about the changes advocated in this book. Though the federal government must carry most of the burden in research and development for new school designs and new school systems, and transitional dollars to help systems move toward these new models, states must play a crucial role. In particular, you can incentivize and support pioneering public districts that want to move in these new directions. At very low costs to the taxpayers of your state, you could fund "transition grants" for both large and small districts that "mirror" transition grants provided by the federal government.

Equally important, you can use the power of your bully pulpits to support this movement and to urge federal involvement.

The states that most aggressively adopt these new approaches will see the fastest results. And as any governor knows, quality education is at the top of the list when it comes to the future economic development of a state.

Sincerely,
Chris Whittle

The Honorable George W. Bush
President
United States of America
cc: Margaret Spellings, Secretary of Education

Dear Mr. President:

The passage of No Child Left Behind under your leadership marked an important chapter in the history of American education. Congratulations on this historic legislation. You moved our schools into an era of accountability that will, when fully implemented, provide schools and teachers the data they need to adapt instruction, allocate resources, and drive higher achievement. NCLB brought additional resources, including additional tutoring to children in failing schools. And finally, the act shines a bright light on the shameful U.S. achievement gap, allowing no school or system to hide behind good averages while groups of children, generally those of poverty or color, do not receive what they deserve and what we promised them. You are to be congratulated for what you have already done for American education. And I should note that it serves as a crucial foundation for future, important changes.

I hope that your administration will add one final act to your educational accomplishments, one that, at the very least, will stand side by side with the importance of NCLB and that potentially will be viewed as a vision that changed the course of U.S. education history.

During your administration, and, I believe, spurred by NCLB, we have already begun to see proficiency rates climb. For example, the Council of the Great City Schools reported in 2004 that major urban districts were posting some of the most impressive gains in years. But it is clear to me that we are going to see something else happen in the three remaining years of your tenure. As you know, NCLB calls for increasing levels of proficiency in *every* year between now and 2014, at which time 100 percent of our school-age children are required to be proficient. Said another way, each year the bar is raised on schools and their students to move the nation toward 100 percent literacy and numeracy. Though I expect overall progress (as measured by proficiency rates) to continue to rise in our public schools during the remainder of your administration, I also predict (as do thousands of others involved in public education) that increasing numbers of schools are not going to be able to achieve the standards you have set. Already, thousands of U.S. schools are failing under NCLB standards. It would not surprise me if that number increases to more than half of all U.S. schools by the end of your term or shortly thereafter.

You know that when this occurs, there will be an outcry. Some will say that NCLB was nothing more than a Republican plot to embarrass and destroy public education. More moderate voices will not go there, but they could well say this: Lower the standards in the act. Neither of those is, in my opinion, the right response.

When NCLB shows that a large percentage of our schools are not performing as we would like and as we should expect, neither embarrassment nor lowering of standards should be our response. The appropriate reaction should be to thank NCLB for enlightening us. What NCLB will be showing us is this: despite all of public education's best efforts, we are finding it impossible to get where we need to be. That is not a failure of our effort. It is not a failure of our commitment. It is a signal that our tried-and-true, but also old and tired, design of schools (most core facets of which are centuries old) and the structure of our school systems *have reached their limits*. NCLB will be discovering educational mental fatigue.

For that reason, we need your help, Mr. President. It is within your power to jump-start research and development on the next era of schools and school systems, the ones that *can* and will achieve the standards you set with NCLB. It is within your power to provide the assistance that will be needed by districts to transition to these new models. This is, in fact, a natural extension of the NCLB Act.

A blueprint of what this plan might be is included in this book. It is one view, and of course there is no one right way to approach this. But approach it we must.

If there are no funds for education R&D, then I hope you will seriously consider reallocating some of the operating funds already being spent in K–12. There will be those who scream about that, but the screams will be louder if more and more of our schools are deemed failing. Some will say it is not the role of the federal government to dive so deeply into K–12. I hope you will remind them that nothing proposed here is being imposed on states or locales, only made available. And I hope you will say to them that it *is* the federal government's role to intervene when our national interest is at risk, which is clearly the case with 30 percent illiteracy rates.

President Roosevelt brought us Social Security. President Eisenhower signed the Interstate Highway Act. President Kennedy sent us to the moon. President Johnson championed the Civil Rights Act. You have a chance to bring America the finest schools on the globe—and to see them graduating students within your lifetime.

Sincerely,
Chris Whittle

An Open Letter to Parents of Children in Underachieving Public Schools

I have saved the most important letter for last.

In the letters that precede this, I have asked the great and powerful to support dramatic change in our system of public education. Some of them will. But they will not succeed without your help.

That's because the most potent advocacy for change comes not from the few people like me who are in public office or who hold positions in schools or education companies, but rather from the collective efforts of parents.

Parents are public education's most selfless stakeholders. You don't seek anything for yourselves at all. You're not looking for more money from a school district, or better job conditions, or reelection to public office. All you want is what is best for your children. Yet the truth is, public education policy is not always driven by what is best for the kids. This is not because the people who run it are evil. It is because the people who run it are *people*. It would be humanly impossible for all the adults who work in public education to prevent their own self-interests, their fears, their egos, and their insecurities from intruding into their perceptions and positions. I'm sure it is true of me, and in ways I cannot always detect and overcome. Some remarkable public educators do so. But most cannot. Just as most of us could not do so in our own careers. We shouldn't expect otherwise of them.

That's why parents are such a critical component in the improvement of public education. They are the counterbalance. They are the "special interest" whose only interest is children. And they have been the drivers of some of the most important changes in public education today. The charter-school movement, for instance, exists because determined parents decided they did not have to accept rampant failure in so many of our nation's schools. And thousands upon thousands of children have brighter futures now as a result.

But too many parents routinely accept schools that are failing their children catastrophically, schools where the vast majority of children are not even at "basic" levels in reading and math—the fundamental building blocks of all knowledge and learning. Too many parents either don't know where their school stands or have come to believe that this is just the way it has to be.

How do we change this tragedy? First, you must believe and know that when children fail, their schools fail, too. The evidence is irrefutable. All children can learn, and all schools can succeed. We see it every day. All we must do to make it happen is to refuse, as a nation, to accept such failure. Every time our nation has done so, we have succeeded—many times in instances when there was no great certainty of success. Here, we *know* it can happen, because it's happening in schools all across the country.

My request is not that you support the specific changes I advocate in this book, though I would welcome your support if you agree. Rather, my request is simply that you engage as relentless advocates for better schools for children. School-board elections typically draw some of the lowest voter turnout in our democracy. My request is that you walk into the voting booth as an accountability taskmaster, a voter who will impose a ruthless electoral accountability upon all those who do not drive strong improvement in our lagging schools—at every level of government.

Whenever a change is proposed, whenever a new idea is debated, let the officials of your schools and your public education system know that you demand improvement and that they will be held accountable for delivering it. Particularly, let them know this when they appear ready to choose to reject change, for this is where the self-interest of adults most frequently is asserted. Put little stock in those who say they are for kids. We all are. Put everything on the results they deliver. No excuses.

Chris Whittle

T here are many numbers in this book related to K–12 education and other sectors. I have chosen not to include foot-
notes throughout, as I think that they would distract from the
concepts being presented. However, in the interest of complete-
ness I share here sources for some of the key information used in
Crash Course.

First, and most important, you may want to know how I calcu-
lated the number of underserved children in America's public
schools at 15 million. Obviously this is an estimation, although I
think those people closest to public education will readily agree
that the number is in that zone—and unconscionably large. To
demonstrate the magnitude of the problem, I averaged the number of students scoring below basic in math and reading for
grades 4 and 8 on the most recent National Assessment of Educational Progress (NAEP) tests. The result was roughly 30 percent.
I then applied that to the approximately 50 million children in U.S.
public schools. Is this a precise number? No. But clearly, Ameri-

can students' achievement—or lack thereof—on this federal test provides a good basis for the magnitude of the problem.

Next, figures for the K–12 public school world in general—total annual expenditures, number of school districts, total schools, students in those schools, and so on—were taken from the *Digest of, Educational Statistics 2003*, published in December 2004 by the National Center for Education Statistics of the U.S. Department of Education. Much of the "final" data included here are from the 2000–2001 school year, with some "estimated" data for the 2001–2002 year and some more current survey results. As appalling as it is in this world of instantaneous electronic transfer of information—but for many good and valid reasons—definitive statistics in the education world are slow to make it into print. So, for the record, the education numbers included here are three or four years old, in contrast to corporate numbers, which are current. I don't think that affects any of the points I've made. In case you were wondering, I chose the *Digest* as my education Bible because it is a comprehensive and well-acknowledged governmental information source. Moreover, for the most part, the data don't change too wildly year to year, although generally the expenditure numbers creep relentlessly higher each year.

Now that I've pegged my source for education statistics and dated it, you should further know that when it comes to K–12 spending on public education, I chose to use the all-in "total" number, which includes capital and debt service as well as operating expenses. Because the treatment of capital expenses can vary from year to year, some education analysts prefer to use the lower "operating" expense numbers. I understand that view but wanted to focus here on the total number, as that is important to understanding the big picture in education. Additionally, the "per pupil" expenditure number that I use throughout the book is run off of "total" expenditures versus "current" expenditures, and enroll-ment in the fall of a school year versus average daily attendance.

One exception to my use of data from the *Digest* is the charter school information included here. The charter school movement is a rapidly growing phenomenon, and to capture this, I have used data for the 2004–2005 school year from the Center for Education Reform, which aggressively tracks changes in this arena.

Finally, I refer several times to a RAND Corporation study of academic achievement gains over time in Edison's schools. This study was scheduled for release in the summer of 2005.

Acknowledgments

M any individuals have helped me extensively with this book
as supporters, critics, readers, editors, fact-checkers, en-
dorsers, and more. Inevitably, any list will fail to include everyone,
and for that, I apologize in advance. I would like to acknowledge
Priscilla Rattazzi Whittle, Laura Eshbaugh, Tim Reeves, Adrian
Zackheim, Julie Grau, Cindy Spiegel, Ed Victor, Chris Cerf, John
Chubb, Steve Wilson, Tung Le, Adam Tucker, Joel Markowitz,
John Danielson, Matt Miller, Walter Isaacson, Rick Stengel, Tom
Ridge, Wendy Kopp, Rod Paige, Lamar Alexander, Tom Ingram,
Nicholas Callaway, Charlie Moss, Susan Calhoun, Tony Kiser,
Beth Alexander, Catherine Bonde, Jan Lippert, Kristal Shipe, and
Kathy Geller Myers.

Also, I must take this opportunity to pay special tribute to the
following:

- *The children attending both the schools Edison manages and the various school-based programs we provide.* You never fail to amaze me with your creativity and potential.

- *The parents who have entrusted their children to Edison's care.* You have taken action on behalf of your children. I appreciate your confidence.

- *The principals, teachers, and staff who selflessly devote their time to the children in Edison's schools and programs.* You understand that the schoolhouse and classroom are where the rubber meets the road in American education—and you take your role to challenge and inspire those kids very seriously.

- *Edison's clients, who have believed that our educational programs could make a difference in the lives of the children they serve.* I especially thank the very early adopters who gave Edison its start. You took a chance on an untested new company and type of business. Your boldness helped pave the way for the idea we represent.

- *Edison's staff, current and past.* You joined up not just for a job but also for a mission. I thank you, everyone. I am constantly amazed at the long hours you work and the incredible energy you put into everything you do on behalf of the children we serve. We can't pay you enough—and don't.

- *Edison's investors.* From the original general partners in Whittle Communications, to the venture capitalists and angels who were there when we opened our first schools, to the equity players who fueled our growth as a private company, invested in us when we were public, and took us private again. There are many ways people can choose to invest their money. A hallmark of our private investors—large and small, early and recent—and our large holders when we were public has been a shared view that one can do well by doing good. Our investors have been eager to learn about education and to help us find ways to better serve America's children.

- *My colleagues from Whittle Communications.* Our work there was (almost) always fun and stimulating. Our successes—and our failures—introduced me to America's public schools and gave me the opportunity to find my true life's work.
- *The Etowah Public School District.* As a product of a rural Southern school system, I owe much of what I have achieved to a host of dedicated teachers in my elementary school, middle school, and high school.

Thanks to all of you.

INDEX

ABOUT THE AUTHOR

After a twenty-five-year career in the media world as the founder of Whittle Communications, owner of *Esquire* magazine, and creator of Channel One, Chris Whittle turned his attention to education with the formation of Edison Schools in 1991. Edison now serves more than 270,000 students in the United States and Great Britain.